MW00612855

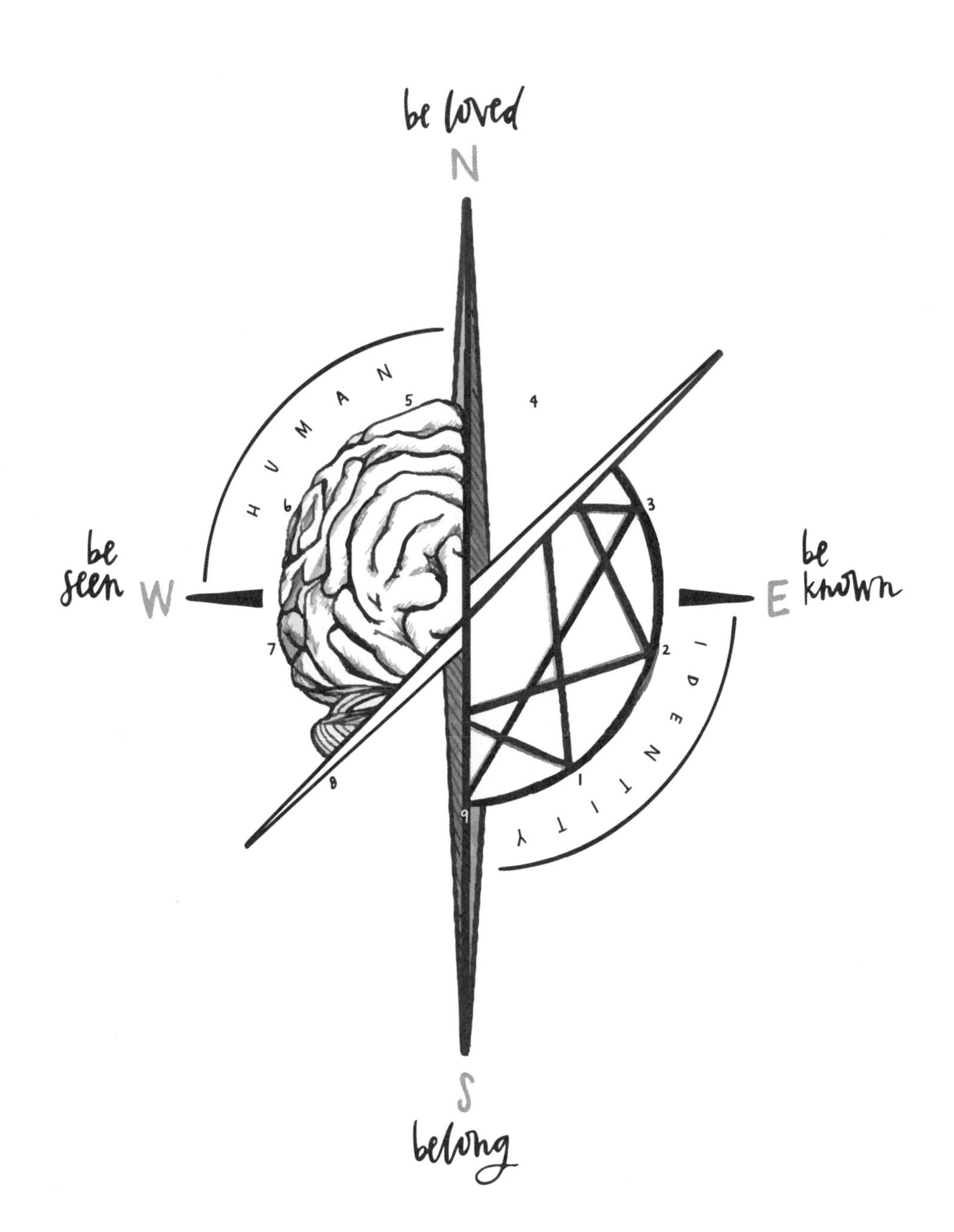
be loved
N
be
seen
W
E
be
known
S
belong
HUMAN
IDENTITY
1
2
3
4
5
6
7
8
9

PRAISE FOR *THE BRAIN-BASED ENNEAGRAM™*

"Whether you consider yourself an expert in the Enneagram or are only beginning to dip your toes in these waters, this book is for you. It is different from anything I have encountered in the arena of wholeness studies and I have personally found it profoundly helpful. Dr. Lubbe is a brilliant innovator as well as a skilled neuro-therapist, and now offers every person a path toward wholeness that is as respectful to the old wisdom of the Elders as it is to current neuroscience."

- Paul Young, author *The Shack*, *Cross Roads*, *Eve* and *Lies We Believe About God*

"Dr. Lubbe literally turns the Enneagram upside down as he introduces readers to a new way of thinking about this ancient wisdom. His work gives me much to think about. If you're an Enneagram student, I'm sure the same will be true for you."

- Suzanne Stabile, author *The Path Between Us* and *The Road Back to You*

"The Enneagram of Personality is more popular than ever, and there are a ton of books out there seeking to unpack its enigmas. *The Brain-Based Enneagram* by Dr. Jerome D. Lubbe makes it into that rare category of essential Enneagram reading.

If you're a seasoned 'Ennea pro' coming from an established tradition, *The Brain-Based Enneagram* is going to deepen your appreciation and application of your path by seamlessly updating you on the latest findings in neuroscience and brain-modeling; drawing surprising (and non-clichéd) parallels to relationships between the Enneagram's nine centers of gravity and everyday life patterns + habits, in both health and hubris.

If you're brand-new to this whole world and want to see what all the fuss is about, *The Brain-Based Enneagram* is an entirely fitting first Enneagram book, because you're going to gain a concise, clear explanation of this symbol as a powerful tool of transformation, rather than just another way to pigeon-hole ourselves. You'll come away seeing how as whole beings, we contain and express all nine numbers in an invitation to one life well-lived.

No matter where you're at in your Enneagram journey, *The Brain-Based Enneagram* is an elegant, energizing guide. Highly recommended."

- Mike Morrell, writer, MikeMorrell.org; co-founder, EnneagramJewelry.com; collaborating author with Richard Rohr, *The Divine Dance: The Trinity and Your Transformation*

"In a world that is constantly underscoring our deficits it is at once refreshing and hopeful to find an approach to healing reminding us that, actually, we are already whole. Appealing to those who understand that how we do anything is how we do everything, now an application of the Enneagram suggests that there is also an integrated and tangible way in which everything also heals, starting with our brain. This work is for people - people striving to support the masses of those to whom things have happened that should never have happened. Dr. Lubbe's approach is anything but topical, the results, swift and lasting."

- Susan Olesek, Founder Enneagram Prison Project & The Human Potentialists

"As the popularity of the Enneagram continues to grow, and this tool for growth makes its way into the common discourse, there is an increased need for literature and resources which help us explore the Enneagram with curiosity, rigour, and compassion. Lubbe's book invites us into a generous and well grounded look at what it means to be human both through insight into the Enneagram and the human brain. Together his rich knowledge of them both creates an opportunity for all of us to see ourselves, and experience ourselves, as whole."

- Hillary L McBride, PhD, author *Mothers, Daughters, and Body Image*

THE BRAIN-BASED ENNEAGRAM™:
you are not A number

BY DR. JEROME D. LUBBE

The Brain-Based Enneagram™

ISBN 978-1-7332945-2-2 (hardcover)
ISBN 978-1-7332945-0-8 (paperback)
ISBN 978-1-7332945-1-5 (ebook)

Written in collaboration with Tiffany Berkowitz
All Artwork, layout and design by Aimee Strickland
Author Photo taken by Sean Champ Smith

2nd edition, 2020 / Printed in the United States of America

TABLE OF CONTENTS

ACKNOWLEDGEMENTS & DISCLAIMERS

ACKNOWLEDGMENTS

My attempt to acknowledge those who have influenced this effort and body of work will undoubtedly be incomplete. I will do my best.

First and foremost is the shade of my heart, my wife, Deborah. She is the anchor by which I have remained present in every sense of the word. This work and my presence would not exist if it weren't for your friendship, partnership, sacrifice, grace, and resolute love. Your courage and companionship inspires me.

To my family and friends. Your encouragement, critique, questions, and conversations have pushed me to refine, iterate and, especially, distill this work. Again and again.

To Tiffany and Aimee, this white paper would not have been created if it weren't for your profound gifts, commitment, and passion for this project. Every single person who is moved by what they read and see here have you to thank. Truly.

The Enneagram authors, experts, mentors, and teachers who laid the profound and life-altering groundwork that influenced this work are many. In alphabetical order they include: A.G.E. Blake, Cynthia Bourgeault, Beatrice Chestnut, David Daniels, G.I. Gurdjeff, Christopher Heuertz, Russ Hudson, Oscar Ichazo, John Luckovich, Mike Morrell, Claudio Naranjo, Helen Palmer, Don Richard Riso, Richard Rohr, and Suzanne Stabile.

WHOLE-IDENTITY VISION

The goal of this work is to foster physical, mental, emotional, and relational health for the purpose of spiritual well-being by increasing self-awareness and practical application via the Whole-Identity Model.

DISCLAIMERS

Clinical

The information shared by Jerome D. Lubbe DC, DACNB is for educational purposes and is not intended to replace professional advice you receive from your doctor. You should always consult with your clinician before starting a healthcare-based regimen of any kind. This information is not to be used to diagnose or treat any condition. Jerome D. Lubbe DC, DACNB is not liable for how you use and implement the information you receive.

Content

Artistic license has been taken with phrases commonly used within the Enneagram community. This has been done with the goal of providing contemporary and Functional Neurology language to previously used terminology in order to create cohesion between neuroscience and the Enneagram. Any utilization of language as it relates to specific schools of thought as it relates to the Enneagram, unless expressly stated, are unintended and coincidental.

Methodology and Concepts

The methodology in this white paper volume is not designed to replace, negate, or contradict existing schools of thought within the Enneagram community. Rather, to provide perspective and a new resource by which existing languages, methods, and understandings can be reinforced, legitimized, integrated, and expanded. Ultimately, the Brain-Based Model of the Enneagram is an innovative and dynamic translation tool for integrating physical, mental, emotional, relational, and spiritual growth through the universal common denominator of brain function.

WE ARE INNATELY
CAPABLE OF WHOLENESS.
THIS IS NOT ABOUT BEING
LESS BROKEN. IT IS ABOUT
BECOMING MORE WHOLE.

The Whole-Identity Profile is not intended to provide answers, but to ask better questions.

PART ONE

NEUROSCIENCE AND THE ENNEAGRAM

WHOLE-IDENTITY PROFILE

The desire and ability to live abundantly well is not limited to one gender, race, class, culture, religion, or any other distinguishing element of who we are. It is universal and all-inclusive. Everyone wants the opportunity to flourish, to grow, to be the best possible version of themselves, and while we are all unique and distinct individuals, often requiring specialized resources for healing and improvement, every single human on the planet has at least one thing in common that drives the process of our becoming wholly well: A brain. This is no small thing we share in. Our development, our decision-making, our thoughts, emotions, actions, and on and on--all reside primarily in the brain. Though our unique, lived experiences shape us differently, we operate within the same system. If we understand how the universal operating system works, we can function with greater success.

The Brain-Based Enneagram offers a unified method for growth to all people. **It is essentially the traditional model(s) of the Enneagram combined with the function of the brain.** It is (w)holistic in its approach, combining the mental, emotional, and physical human experiences simultaneously. These three components make up who we are--and they are mirrored in both the Enneagram intelligence centers (instinct, intuition, intellect triads) and in brain anatomy (brain-stem, right hemisphere, left hemisphere). By integrating the psychological model of the Enneagram with neuroscience, we build a Brain-Based model that approaches personal development (w)holistically and practically, affording ourselves the best possible chance at flourishing.

The following conversation begins with a 30,000 foot view of the Brain-Based Enneagram where we skim the surface of neuroscience, cover the basics of the Enneagram, and explore how the two systems intersect to build a more inclusive, reliable, and applicable model for growth. At 1,000 feet we dig further into the specific components of the Brain-Based model. At 10 feet we discuss how to score and apply the new model of the Enneagram to our lives. Next, we explore practical steps for growth in each number. Finally, we revisit the 30,000 foot perspective to imagine the implications and possibilities of the Brain-Based Enneagram moving forward.

As with any new concept, this is only the start. There is still much to be discovered, much to be discussed, and much to be lived. Let's begin.

THE NEUROPSYCHOLOGY OF IDENTITY

You are not a *personality*. You are not even multiple personalities. You *have an identity*--and what creates and characterizes your identity can be charted by the nine numbers of the Enneagram. The anatomy of the brain reflects this: We are not left-brained or right-brained, we are whole-brained. The same is true for the Enneagram. To put it more plainly, you are not a personality type or a number on the Enneagram. **You are a whole person who has a whole identity--you are all nine numbers.** Just like you have a *whole brain*, you also have a *whole identity*. Tools like the Enneagram are meant for expanding awareness of the whole. The nine numbers of the Enneagram offer a language and a system for understanding and discussing the diverse landscape of everything that makes you who you are. Neuroscience provides a way of connecting this language and system to your very own internal operating system: Your brain.

Your identity is the sum total of every good and every bad thing that has ever happened to you, including genetics.

Your identity, formed in the brain, is comprised of nature, nurture, *and* discipline collectively. It is shaped by your combined life experiences--both positive and negative--as limbic attachments develop. These limbic attachments, in response to your experiences, create distinct behaviors, patterns, attachments, and associations. Through neuroplasticity, with the help of tools like the Brain-Based Enneagram, you can reshape and remake how your brain not only functions, but how it continues to develop into the future.

> "Any man could, if he were so inclined, be the sculptor of his own brain."
>
> - *Santiago Ramon y Cajal*

THE NEUROSCIENCE

Brain anatomy and brain function are rich with complexity. We cannot cover everything in one pass, but we can examine a high-level view of how the three main areas of our brain (brainstem, right hemisphere, and left hemisphere) develop and operate together. We will use a pie chart (not unlike the Enneagram) to represent these components and discuss their relationship to each other. By starting with the brain, we lay a foundation for the Brain-Based Enneagram.
As the discussion progresses, we'll add layers to the diagram in order to connect the neuroscience with the nine numbers of the Enneagram.

BRAIN-STEM

BRAIN-STEM

The brain-stem is the first component of the brain to bloom. It is responsible for driving the instinctual nature of humanity. Years and years of life on this planet have given our species a hard-wired set of skills for survival. In our most primal state, every single human on earth is--at any given moment, whether we know it or not--moving towards pleasure and/or away from pain. It is biologically hard-wired within us to seek pleasure and avoid pain. They are metrics for survival! Pain bad, Pleasure good. And as with any living species, we want to survive, so we follow our gut.

The brain-stem generates your reactive gut-response by sending signals to your body before your brain is able to comprehend or process the incoming information. It is the autonomic nervous system, and it is responsible for keeping you alive. The brain-stem is not built for sophisticated mental or emotional processing--it is built for action-based instinct. This is important because in matters of life or death, a quick response makes all the difference.

Within the brain-stem are the midbrain, pons, and medulla. The midbrain is responsible for the fight or flight system (sympathetic system), and the pons and medulla make up what is called the PMRF (pontomedullary reticular formation) which is the "rest and digest" system (parasympathetic system). This means the brain-stem is constantly regulating between "fight and flight" and "rest and digest", which are both *instinctual* functions. This is why it corresponds with the gut triad of the Enneagram (more on that later).

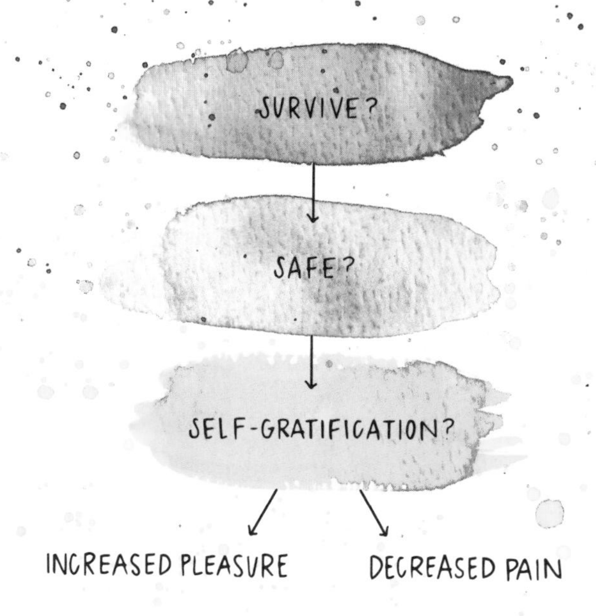
INNATE SUBCONSCIOUS
INSTINCTIVE DECISION-MAKING
SURVIVE?
SAFE?
SELF-GRATIFICATION?
INCREASED PLEASURE
DECREASED PAIN

LIMBIC ATTACHMENTS

Self-gratification has two avenues: Increased pleasure and/or Decreased pain. When you're trying to survive, you want to both increase positive (life-giving) experiences and decrease negative (potentially life-threatening) experiences. To do so, your brain goes through a subconscious three-step process for making decisions about survival. It asks:

1. Am I going to survive?
2. If I am not in a life-threatening situation, am I safe?
3. What form of self-gratification will allow me to maintain what I have learned to consider *safety*, how am I going to achieve self-gratification?

The process of moving towards pleasure and away from pain increases your chance of survival and subconsciously feeds information to your brain, which then impacts your mental, emotional, and physical development. Neuroscience tells us that 3-5% of your brain is conscious, and everything else (95-97% of brain activity) is subconscious. Most of this subconscious activity is driven by the brain-stem, and thanks to subconscious limbic attachments, the survival strategies you employ (which ultimately shape your identity) are the result of every good and every bad thing that has ever happened to you, including your genetics. That means 95-97% of your identity is formed on a subconscious level.

RISK (-)

Absence of positive experiences
Presence of negative experiences

Three primary factors that generate limbic attachments are:

Intensity: *How strong is the experience?*
Duration: *How long does it last?*
Frequency: *How often does it happen?*

Essentially, limbic attachments transfer short-term information to subconscious long-term memory. The stronger the experience, the more intense the transfer. The longer the experience, the more sustained the transfer. The more frequent the experience, the more persistent the transfer. All of our limbic attachments are created based on varying combinations of these three experiences (strong, long and often). That means our most profound positive experiences (reward) and our most profound negative experiences (trauma) are the most identity-shaping experiences we have--and that most of them are being formed without our conscious awareness.

When something (positive or negative) happens strong enough, long enough, or often enough, our brain creates a limbic attachment to that experience. Our survival strategies are then rewired in the wake of the new association, and along with it our identities--to an extent--are rewired as well. For example, when 9/11 happened in the United States, not only was it an extraordinarily intense experience, but the impact lasted for a long time, and news coverage kept the event frequently on our minds. 9/11 created a global limbic attachment. Politics aside, it was traumatic in intensity, duration, *and* frequency--and this shifted the identity of the entire nation.

Even if a traumatic event doesn't actually last long or happen often, the brain is prone to believe it is reliving and re-experiencing our powerful memories. When this happens, the brain perceives the frequency and duration to be high--and in matters of the brain, perception is reality. A limbic attachment is likely to occur.

It is important to note that limbic experiences are not only negative--they are also positive. Increased pleasure creates positive limbic attachments, and decreased pain creates positive limbic attachments. When raised in a life-giving environment where a reward-cycle was nurtured, positive limbic attachments are formed. Imagine a spectrum of risk and reward:

These are the metrics the brain-stem measures for survival. Identity is formed in the process of navigating risk and reward as the events of our life unfold. Who we become is a product of this identity-making process.

REWARD (+)

Presence of positive experiences
Absence of negative experiences

WHOLE BRAIN

The right hemisphere is the second system to come online during development. It is responsible for processing compound emotions, imagination and creative flow states, empathy, and so on. Because of the right brain, you experience form, music, color, and abstract language. None of this happens without the integration of the left hemisphere and the brain-stem, but the right brain does the heavy lifting for complex felt-experiences. In contrast to the brain-stem, your right hemisphere is not about instinct, but about intuition.

Subconsciously and consciously, you gather complex emotional experiences and fit them together to form a worldview that exists outside of rational language. This process begins at a young age and continues into adulthood. This is essential for development. Imagine a life whereby the only metrics you could use for decision-making were intellectual data and/or gut instinct. No emotional perspective, no heart, no fine-

LEFT HEMISPHERE

tuned receptors fit to feel the energy beneath the action. Intuition is our emotional language, and emotion is a vital access point for rewiring the brain for health.

The third component to fully develop is the left hemisphere. This side of your brain is responsible for complex thought and control of emotions, analysis, logical reasoning, etc. In partnership with the right hemisphere and the brain-stem, the left hemisphere enables you to communicate richly, solve complex problems, and generate systems. It is not driven by instinct or intuition, but by intellect.

It is by intellect that we can even have this exchange of ideas. Intellect is the pattern built from data and observation. It is what enabled humanity to scale the food chain so rapidly, and is a valuable tool for improving mental, emotional, and physical well-being. By way of intellect, we can present data to ourselves in order to shape a healthier perceived reality, thus creating a healthier lived reality.

There is no truth to the myth of *being* a "right brained" or "left brained" person. Although the right hemisphere is tethered to intuition, the left is tethered to intellect, and the brain-stem is tethered to instinct, your preference of one function over the other doesn't mean *you are* one over the other. You have a whole brain, which means you have all three components--the brain-stem, the right hemisphere, and the left. Together, they integrate to form what ultimately shapes your identity.

THE ENNEAGRAM

A BRIEF HISTORY OF THE ENNEAGRAM AND ITS INFLUENCES

By Mike Morrell and John Luckovich

The Enneagram is is an enigmatic nine-pointed symbol that represents the interaction of energies within a process. It illustrates the relationship between the essential character of a phenomenon and how this character is expressed in sequential stages through time. Today, the Enneagram is most widely recognized and taught as a system of character types that draws from ancient wisdom traditions and insights from modern psychology.

The history of the Enneagram is complex, and in tracing it's lineage, it becomes clear that the Enneagram had many different expressions and stages in its evolution. The current usage and understanding of the Enneagram began with the teachings of George Ivanovich Gurdjieff (1866-1949), an equally enigmatic teacher who was born in the city of Kars in modern-day Turkey close to the Silk Road, where he was influenced by a variety of traditions East and West, later setting out to seek schools of inner wisdom. According to Gurdjieff, he found such wisdom, still preserved in several millennia-old orders and brotherhoods who trace their own roots back to ancient Egypt.

After some years, Gurdjieff began to teach in Russia, Europe, and the United States. It was Gurdjieff's claim that human beings are 'asleep' to their full expression of spirit, will, and being, and that a great many forces - external and internal - conspire to keep us this way. The good news is that waking up is possible, but the keys to our awakening lie in the development of our attention and fostering the right relationship between our Essence, our spiritual core, and our personality.

For this awakening to happen, he said, the three centers of understanding and perception in human beings had to be awakened and functioning properly, rather than left to the disorganized state of the average person. These centers are the body, the heart, and the mind. Gurdjieff recognized that many traditional spiritual paths typically emphasized the development of one of these three centers at the expense of the other two. The way of the *fakir* or ascetic was an attempt to overcome identification with the body. The way of the *monk* could be seen in devotional monastic paths, such as the Eastern Orthodox monastic orders and Sufi Dervish orders he observed, emphasizing a singular focus on the heart center. Paths which disciplined attention and understanding, such as Indian Yogis and Zen monks, cultivated the *mind*. Further, most expressions of these three paths require that one give up their life as a 'householder' or regular participator in work, family, and society, instead retreating from the world to live in solitude or a spiritual order. Gurdjieff called his work the *Fourth Way* because he sought means of developing all three centers, and within the conditions of daily life.

The Enneagram was taught by Gurdjieff as a 'universal hieroglyph' of this Fourth Way, symbolizing the joining together and interaction of what Gurdjieff called the Law of One, the Law of Three, and the Law of Seven. These laws are seen as universal, finding representation in nearly every spiritual tradition worldwide.

The Law of One is, simply, that everything emerges from one source. The Law of Three, reflected by innumerable trinities in spiritual traditions worldwide, describes how any whole phenomenon manifests in three aspects: an active, passive, and reconciling force. The Law of Seven represents process and draws from the same principles as the musical octave. It describes how the 'One,' represented in three elements, finds expression in stages through time. For Gurdjieff, the Enneagram wasn't a conceptual tool but a living dynamic system which he illustrated in human movement through sacred dances drawn from Sufi, Tibetan, and other sources, choreographed by Mr. Gurdjieff with aid from his collaborator, the Russian composer Thomas de Hartmann (1885-1956).

The teachings of Gurdjieff are complex and had many stages of evolution through different periods of his life and as his own understanding deepened. Gurdjieff never taught the Enneagram as a personality system, and for many who study the Gurdjieff Work, the modern Enneagram of Personality is considered derivative or even a tool used to reinforce identification with the personality rather than expanding one's ability to see beyond it.

The Enneagram would take another evolutionary leap forward through the efforts of the Bolivian-born, Peruvian-raised teacher Oscar Ichazo (born 1931). Drawing from Gurdjieff, Ichazo combined the Enneagram, the understanding of the centers, and the dynamics between Essence and personality with his understanding of several ancient systems of understanding, including the nine extant manifestations of the Divine as 'Sephriot' in the esoteric Jewish Kabbalistic Tree of Life, the Christian mystic Evagrius Ponticus' early catalogue of human vices (which became the prototype of the Medieval Seven Deadly Sins and Seven Lively Virtues), and the work of Neoplatonists such as Plotinus (in his Enneads) and Proclus. In all, Ichazo claimed to have come up with 108 'Enneagons,' which he taught in his mystical school in Arica, Chile. From these 108 Enneagons, just four make up the basics of the modern Enneagram of Personality: the Passions, the Fixations, the Virtues, and the Holy Ideas, providing an inner map for awakening Essence and seeing (in echoes of Gurdjieff) what psychological patterns keep us 'asleep.'

Ichazo's teachings were elaborate, but our contemporary appreciation of the Enneagram might have never occurred if it had remained in his closely-guarded world: It would take a multidisciplinary student of his to free the Enneagram from its esoteric cage.

Enter Chilean-born psychiatrist, Fulbright scholar, and student of theologian Paul Tillich, Claudio Naranjo (born 1932). Naranjo joined Arica and studied under Ichazo, streamlining Ichazo's teachings and teaching them in North and South America, much to Ichazo's chagrin. Naranjo expanded the application of the Enneagram's intrapersonal wisdom to the interpersonal interactions of entire cultures in his *Enneagram of Society*. Naranjo's work and teaching had a direct influence on many of the modern innovators and teachers of the Enneagram of Personality, including Helen Palmer and Diamond Approach founder A.H. Almaas. One of Naranjo's students, Jesuit Robert Ochs, taught the Enneagram in Christian communities, inspiring the likes of Richard Rohr, Don Riso and his later teaching partner Russ Hudson.

Contemporary Enneagram teachers continue to broaden its impact in psychological, spiritual, educational and organizational domains. The introduction you hold in your hands builds on the work of these pioneering and adapting geniuses, with a particular focus on how contemporary brain science challenges and validates the emergent Enneagram model.

—special thanks to Mike Morrell (enneagramjewelry.com) and John Luckovich (newyorkenneagram.com) for the History of the Enneagram section.

INTELLECT
LEFT HEMISPHERE
INTUITION
RIGHT HEMISPHERE
INSTINCT
BRAIN-STEM

INSTINCT

The Instinct Triad of the Enneagram is where numbers 8, 9, and 1 reside. This triad corresponds with an instinctive nature. When under stress, the nature of this triad defaults to unmitigated primitive emotional reactions (panic, rage, sorrow, hysteria etc.) as the primary survival-based stress response. In the Brain-Based Enneagram, these numbers also correspond with the brain-stem.

Typically, the Enneagram symbol has been drawn with number 9 at the top of the circle. But in the Brain-Based Enneagram, the Instinct triad corresponds with the brain-stem which is at the base of the brain. So the new diagram turns the circle upside-down and anchors number 9 at the bottom. This adjustment comes with several advantages. First, we are able to witness the interconnectedness of the Enneagram the same way we are able to witness the interconnectedness of the three components of the central nervous system, thus providing a more (w)holistic perspective of the

Enneagram. Second, we begin to appreciate how the behaviors and tendencies of numbers 8, 9, and 1 specifically relate to the instinctual, physical elements of who we are, which are primarily developed in the brain-stem. Beyond this, it provides a helpful framework for practically applying neuroscience and the Enneagram to our lives, our relationships, our families, and our work. When we understand which component of the brain is responsible for each efficiency and inefficiency in our Enneagram profile, we can chart a science-based path for personal development.

As a companion of the brain-stem, the Instinct Triad is physical. We can apply this understanding to improve the efficiencies of 8, 9, and 1 by remembering the body as essential to the process of becoming integrated. Knowing and navigating the self is not only a mental or emotional work, it is also deeply physical. The wisdom of our physical self is ancient, just as the brain-stem is the oldest component of the brain. Understanding how to strengthen the function of the brain-stem gives us an actionable system for strengthening our efficiencies in the healthy aspects of 8, 9, and 1 on the Enneagram.

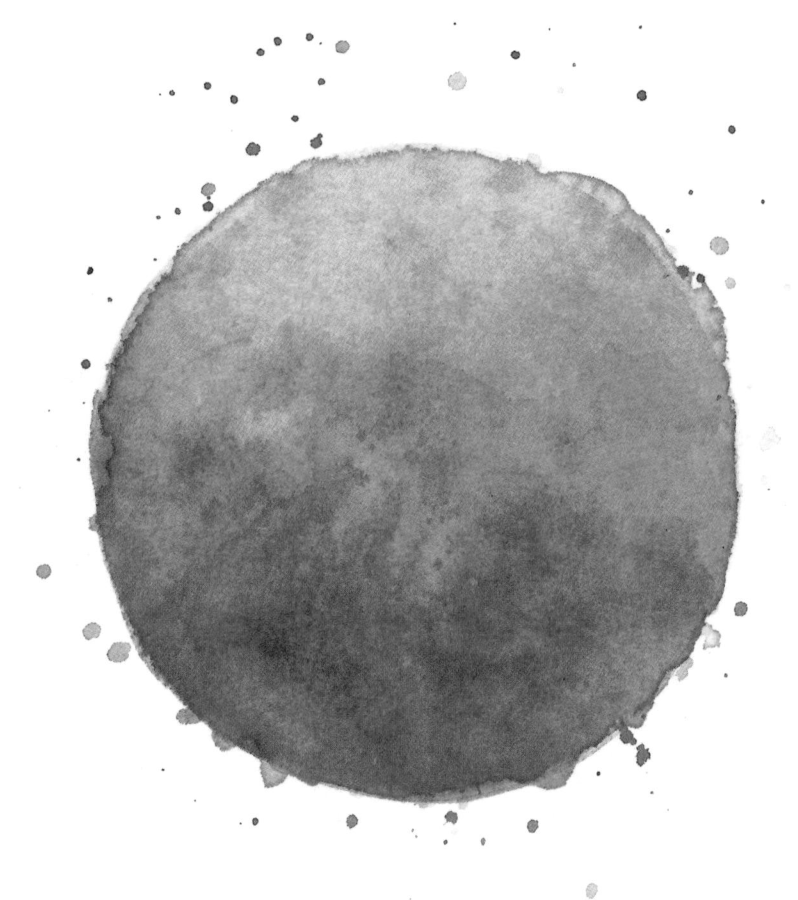

INSTINCT

INTUITION

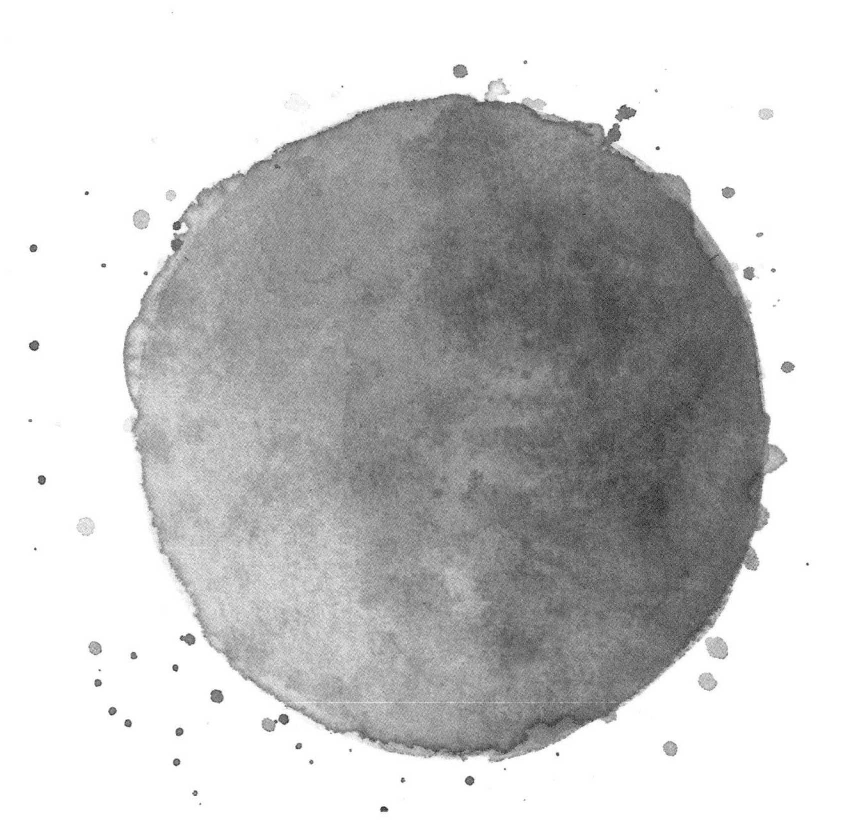

To the upper right is the Intuition Triad, which corresponds with the right hemisphere of the brain. It is the heart center, responsible for complex expressed emotions. When under stress, the nature of this triad defaults to complex expressed emotions such as, but not limited to: joy, shame, guilt, love, mercy, long-suffering, etc. as the primary survival-based stress response. Numbers 2, 3, and 4 exist within the Intuition triad, and are traditionally considered the heart-numbers. By overlapping the right hemisphere of the brain with the Intuition triad of the Enneagram, we can use Functional Neurology to physically strengthen the inefficient areas of our brain and improve our expression of the values and innate capacities associated with numbers 2, 3, and 4.

For example, a person who has efficient 4 energy may be more likely to experience depression. If this person understands the function of the right-hemisphere and can engage in science-based practices designed to strengthen it, they gain access to a legitimate way of improving their emotional health, and thus their overall life experience. Put simply, when you improve the right hemisphere, expressions 2, 3, and 4 produce healthier outcomes.

To the left is the Intellect Triad, associated with the left hemisphere. It exists in relationship to the intellectual nature, and corresponds with complex control of emotions as a survival-based stress response (attention, caution, skepticism, etc). When we understand how to improve the function of the left-hemisphere, we increase efficiencies in the values of numbers 5, 6, and 7.

For example, someone who is inefficient in 7 may have a difficult time playing. A functional map of the brain shows which parts of the brain are engaged during play. By using this information, we can find safe ways of stimulating those areas in order to increase activity in the faculties necessary for allowing play. When the activity of those areas increases, the capacity for play increases, which promotes a healthier efficiency in 7. Essentially, we can hack the Enneagram and improve our efficiency in any of the numbers by applying what we know about neurological function to the values of each number.

INTELLECT

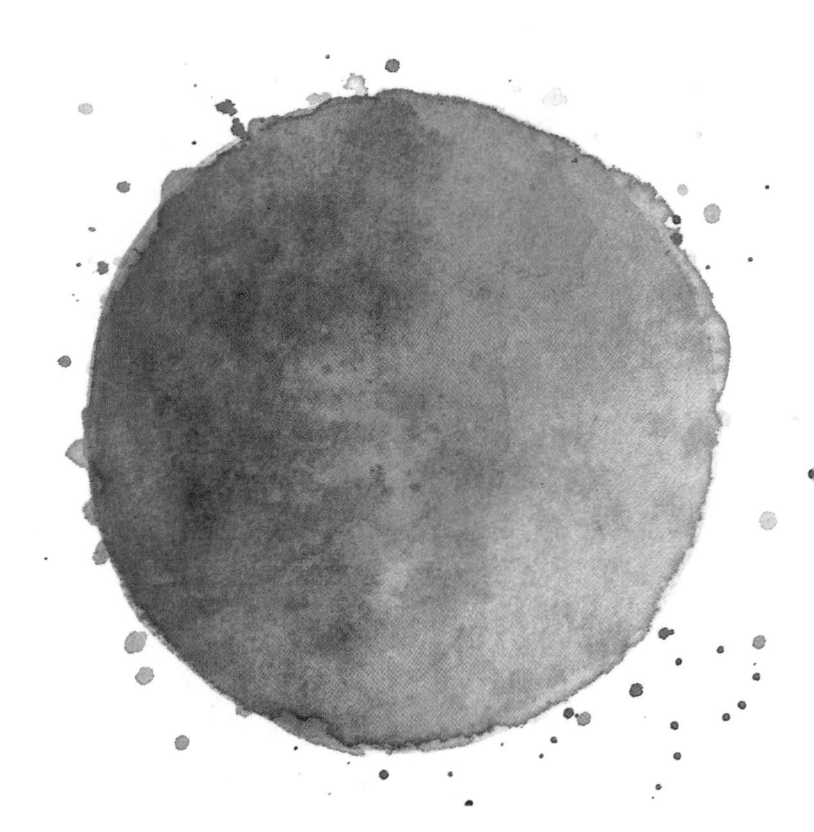

THE BRAIN-BASED ENNEAGRAM

Simply, the Brain-Based Enneagram exists to provide a neuroscience-driven opportunity to use the Enneagram for greater personal, relational, and global thriving. When we understand the Enneagram as a Whole-Identity Profile instead of a single-number personality "type", we expand our capacity for growth and health in a multitude of directions.

...we are able to see how the intersection of Functional Neurology and the Enneagram creates a practical guide for improving (w)holistic well-being.

PART TWO

THE BRAIN-BASED
ENNEAGRAM

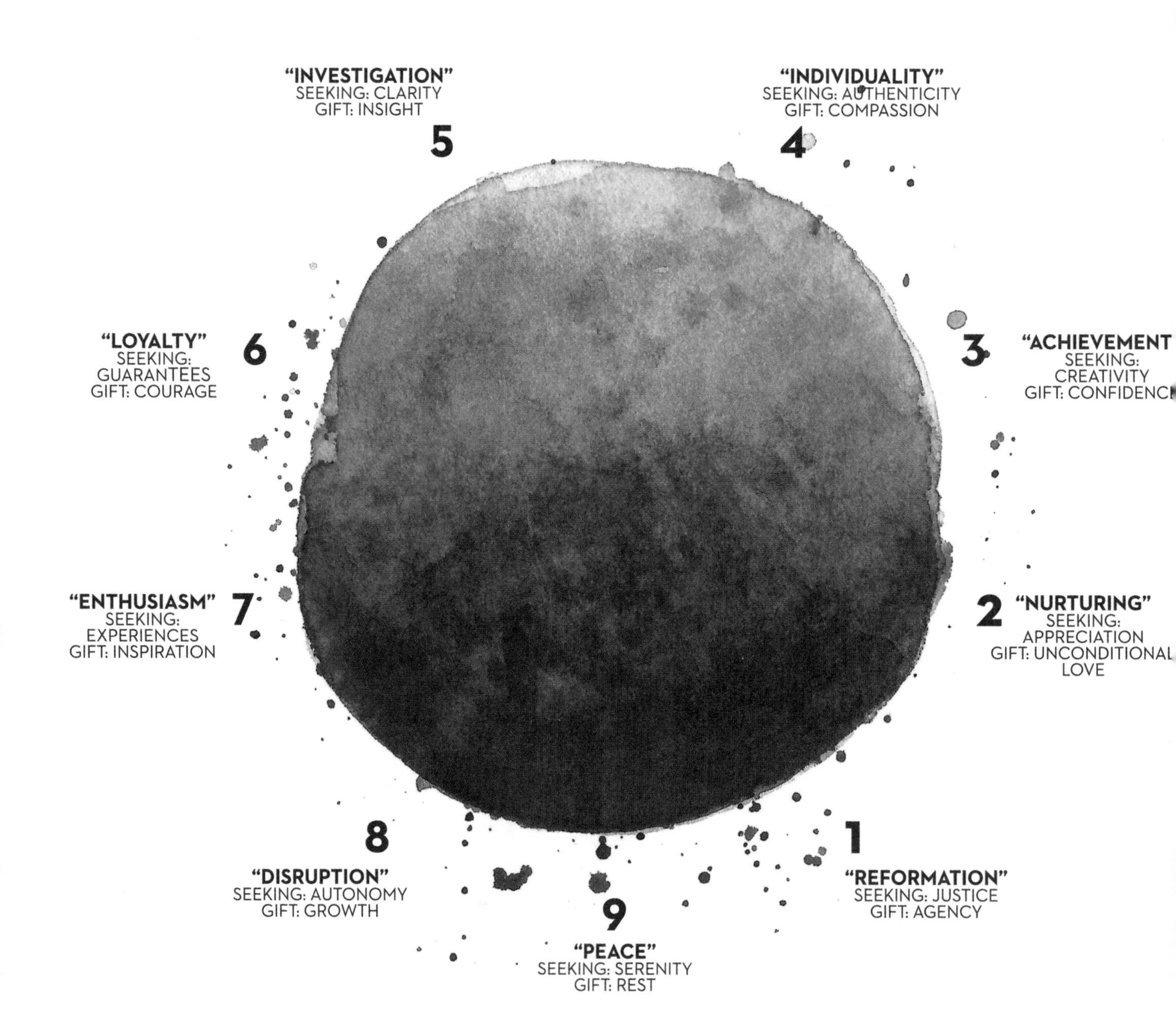

5
"INVESTIGATION"
SEEKING: CLARITY
GIFT: INSIGHT
4
"INDIVIDUALITY"
SEEKING: AUTHENTICITY
GIFT: COMPASSION
6
"LOYALTY"
SEEKING:
GUARANTEES
GIFT: COURAGE
3
"ACHIEVEMENT
SEEKING:
CREATIVITY
GIFT: CONFIDENC
7
"ENTHUSIASM"
SEEKING:
EXPERIENCES
GIFT: INSPIRATION
2
"NURTURING"
SEEKING:
APPRECIATION
GIFT: UNCONDITIONAL
LOVE
8
"DISRUPTION"
SEEKING: AUTONOMY
GIFT: GROWTH
1
"REFORMATION"
SEEKING: JUSTICE
GIFT: AGENCY
9
"PEACE"
SEEKING: SERENITY
GIFT: REST

THE BRAIN-BASED ENNEAGRAM

Until now, there has been no brain-based model of the Enneagram.

To our enormous advantage, observing the Enneagram through the lens of neuroscience expands and integrates the traditional model to provide a way for even greater personal, relational, and global wellness. When we look at the Enneagram in terms of brain function, we do not learn our "personality type", but instead begin to comprehensively understand which parts of the brain are responsible for our behaviors (thoughts, feelings and actions), how they correspond with the values of each of the nine numbers, and what we can practically do to strengthen our efficiencies in all of them. In this way, we craft a customized, (w)holistic growth path for personal development.

ALL NINE NUMBERS

"What is your number?" is the most frequently asked question in regard to the Enneagram. But in the Brain-Based model, we learn to see ourselves as all nine numbers simultaneously, and to consider our efficiency in each.

For example, instead of "I am a 1" you might say, "I have high efficiency in 1" and then perhaps, "my 7 nature is strong as well." That means if you tested as a 1 you would not "be" a 1, but instead would "have high efficiency" in the *nature* of 1. When that is the case, you can further inquire, "...and what is my relationship to the rest of the numbers/natures?" All around the circle, you witness the efficiency or inefficiency with which you utilize each number, and paint a more (w)holistic picture of your personal neuropsychology.

Efficiency in a number means there is an ease of relationship with the nature of that number. It means you engage often. Efficiency by definition is "accomplishing a task with the least amount of allocated resources and energy required". It is important to understand this is not an indication of health, but of ease of use. Someone who enjoys autonomy is going to have high efficiency in 8, but that doesn't mean they *are* an 8. They're multi-faceted. For instance, perhaps they also value clarity and authenticity, so they're efficient in 5 and 4 nature(s) as well. The analysis should be applied to all nine numbers for a more integrated perspective of the whole.

Inefficiency in a number means there is less ease in the relationship with the nature of that number. You don't often engage. It means accomplishing tasks related to inefficient numbers/natures

Every single person has access to all nine numbers. Based on nature, nurture, and discipline, you express the values of each number at varying degrees of intensity based on your lived experience.

requires increased allocation of resources and utilizes a significant amount of energy. Imagine the same person who is efficient in 8 struggles to see the value of serenity and guarantees. They are likely inefficient in 6 and 9. Instead of turning 6 and 9 away as irrelevant, they can instead expand their capacity for greater efficiency.

You are not one thing, you are complex and multifaceted; you are interconnected. This is a vital paradigm shift. When you consider having access to all nine numbers simultaneously, you increase and expand your capacity for thriving.

BRAIN-BASED LANGUAGE

When you shift the Enneagram framework from *being* one number to *having efficiencies* in all nine numbers, the Enneagram language shifts with it. It becomes about *nature* and *values* instead of *type* and *reductive behaviors*. For example number 7, traditionally associated with the title of "Enthusiast", is instead represented by the innate human capacity for "Enthusiasm" as well as the value of "Experiences".

"I am an enthusiast" becomes "I value experiences" which allows more room for nuance, invites growth, and begs the question, "...and what else do I value?"

Brain-Based Enneagram Language

8	I am a *Challenger* =	I value ***Autonomy***
9	I am a *Peacemaker* =	I value ***Serenity***
1	I am a *Reformer* =	I value ***Justice***
2	I am a *Helper* =	I value ***Appreciation***
3	I am an *Achiever* =	I value ***Creativity***
4	I am an *Individualist* =	I value ***Authenticity***
5	I am an *Investigator* =	I value ***Clarity***
6	I am a *Loyalist* =	I value ***Guarantees***
7	I am an *Enthusiast* =	I value ***Experiences***

There is no human who is defined by a single number.

NATURE(S) AND SCORES

If you are all nine numbers, you need a way of measuring your efficiencies in each. Certainly none of us are perfectly balanced in every expression, so how can we assess our Whole-Identity Profile through the Brain-Based Enneagram? By measuring in ways that are already familiar to us: Capacity, Speed, Volume, and Strength.

Pick the ones that resonate most. These four metrics are tools meant to help you visualize the Brain-Based Enneagram and imagine what it means to be a Whole-Identity human. They provide options for language, which provide options for comprehension.

For example:

Capacity "I have high capacity in 8 energy."
Speed "I move quickly in the nature of a 2."
Volume "The volume on my 9 is turned way down."
Strength "I express 1 strongly."
~~*Instead of* "I am a 3"~~

RPM *Capacity*
MPH *Speed*
DB *Volume*
HP *Strength*

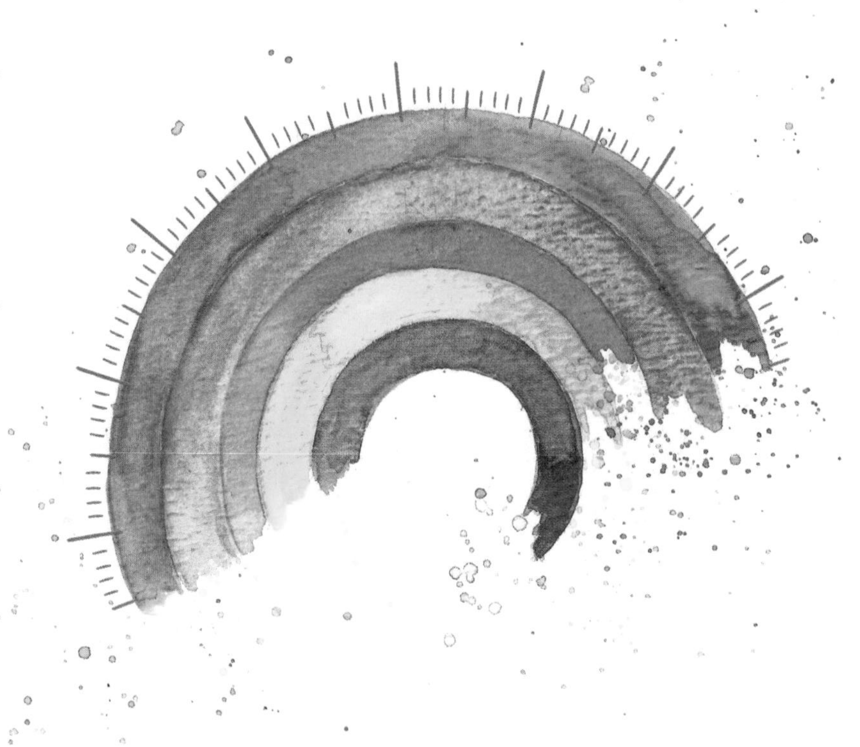

To discover your degrees of efficiency in each number, review your RHETI test results. You will be given a score for each. You'll notice right away that some numbers are associated with a high score (21+), some in the middle (11-20), and some on the low end (1-10).

RHETI RESULTS

NATURE : SCORES

SURVIVAL STRATEGIES / UTILIZATION

EFFICIENCY RATING

____ : ____
____ : ____
____ : ____
____ : ____
____ : ____
____ : ____
____ : ____
____ : ____
____ : ____

DB/MPH HP/RPM

⊕ | USEFUL | SAFE
NEED: ° OF PRESENCE
"LIFE-GIVING"
↑ BUDGETED RESOURCES
↓ TAXES & INTEREST

⊜

↑ TAXES & INTEREST
↓ BUDGETED RESOURCES
"LIFE-THREATENING"
NEED: ° OF ABSENCE
⊝ | USELESS | UNSAFE

DB/MPH HP/RPM

DB: VOLUME, **HP**: STRENGTH,
MPH: SPEED, **RPM**: CAPACITY
⊕ GAS, ⊜ CRUISE, ⊝ BRAKE

POPULATION DENSITY MAP

ALL NINE NUMBERS = GLOBAL
TRIAD = CONTINENT
EACH NUMBER = A COUNTRY
WINGS = FLIGHT PLAN(S)

You are a concert of collective experiences, every instrument played to varying degrees. To comprehend and shape those variables, you need tools. These metrics provide the scales necessary for weighing efficiencies in each expressed nature of the Enneagram.

High-scoring numbers: (High Efficiency): 21+

RPM	High capacity
MPH	Fast speed
DB	High volume
HP	Powerful strength

High-scoring numbers are the expressions you unconsciously find most life-giving. You function most efficiently in the nature of these numbers. From a brain-based perspective, this is because your limbic attachments to these expressions are connected to a self-gratification ratio (pleasure-seeking/pain-avoidant) that reflects an increased chance of survival. Based on your lived experiences, engaging these numbers feel more useful and safe as compared to your low(er) numbers, so you utilize them often.

Mid-scoring numbers: (Average Efficiency): 11-20

RPM	Average capacity
MPH	Neutral speed
DB	Balanced volume
HP	Average strength

Mid-scoring numbers are relatively neutral. You are neither particularly at ease or dis-ease with these expressions as compared to your highest and lowest numbers. You don't consciously rely on their presence, but you don't consciously avoid them either.

Low-scoring numbers: (Low Efficiency): 1-10

RPM	Low capacity
MPH	Slow speed
DB	Low volume
HP	Low strength

From a brain-based perspective, your limbic attachments associated with these expressions are connected to a self-gratification ratio (pleasure-seeking/pain-avoidant) that reflects a decreased chance of survival. Based on your lived experiences, you view them as useless, unsafe, or unrewarding, so you unconsciously avoid and make them absent (to varying degrees). At an extreme, these Enneagram expressions can feel life-threatening. In general, you are not strengthened or efficient in these functions, so you tend not to engage with them.

WINGS

> "Travel is fatal to prejudice, bigotry, and narrow-mindedness, and many of our people need it sorely on these accounts. Broad, wholesome, charitable views of men and things cannot be acquired by vegetating in one little corner of the earth all one's lifetime."
>
> - *Mark Twain*

Each of the nine Enneagram numbers branch off into two more nuanced expressions called "wings". For example, a four branches into a four-wing-three and a four-wing-five. A six branches into a six-wing-five and a six-wing-seven. Each number moves in the direction of their two closest neighbors. Just as we have access to all nine numbers, we also have access to all 18 wings, more or less efficient in each. This means we can learn to increase our efficiencies in not only all nine numbers, but in all 18 wing expressions as well.

The 18 wings are more than individual expressions--they are parts of a whole, and they are in relationship with each other. The interaction between the 18 wings can be compared to a flight map. We become more and more capable of traveling between different wing expressions as we improve the overall health of our whole identity. The conscious and subconscious routes we take are dependent on the destinations we are attempting to reach. When we are optimized, we can maneuver easily through our different natures and efficiencies. This means, again, that we are not one number, we are not one wing (such as a 4w3), but that we are all 9 numbers, all 18 wings, and ultimately, capable of each of these 27 expressions of the Enneagram as a Whole-Identity Profile.

Note: For the sake of brevity, this volume of the Whole-Identity Profile will not dive into the nature of the Instincts (often referred to as sub-types). That effort will be pursued in subsequent volumes.

THE 18 WING RELATIONSHIPS

8w7	*Maverick* Nature	8w9	*Bear* Nature
9w8	*Referee* Nature	9w1	*Dreamer* Nature
1w9	*Idealist* Nature	1w2	*Advocate* Nature
2w1	*Servant* Nature	2w3	*Steward* Nature
3w2	*Charmer* Nature	3w4	*Professional* Nature
4w3	*Influencer* Nature	4w5	*Seeker* Nature
5w4	*Innovator* Nature	5w6	*Problem-Solver* Nature
6w5	*Defender* Nature	6w7	*Companion* Nature
7w6	*Entertainer* Nature	7w8	*Sensationalist* Nature

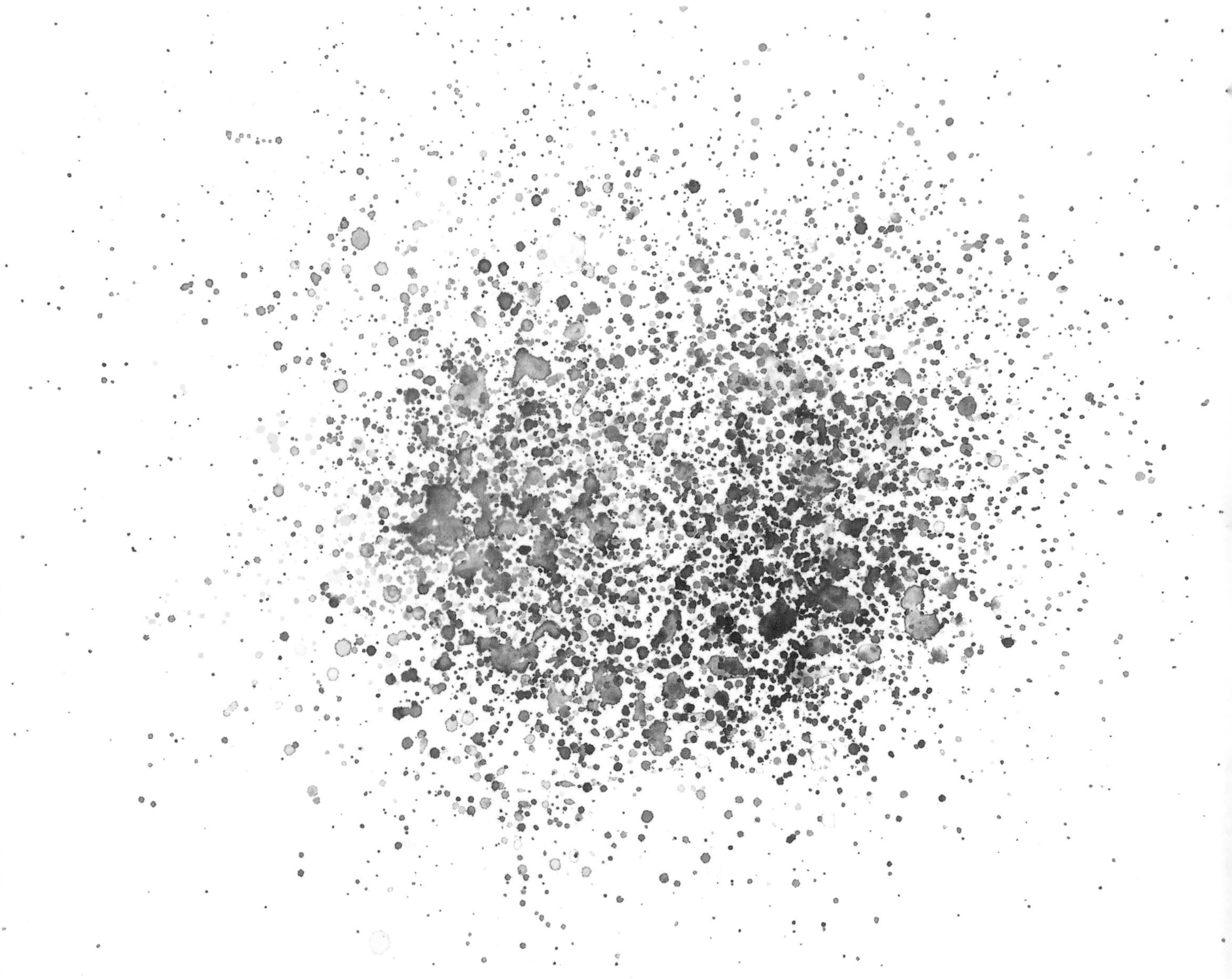

POPULATION DENSITY MAP

Imagine a population density map of the globe. All over the land, there are glowing dots that represent the human population. Some areas are lit up like the sun, and others are scattered thin. Still other areas, like the icy terrain of Greenland, are hardly illuminated at all.

Imagine a population density map of your brain. All over your neurological landscape, there are sparks of activity in the regions you utilize most. Some areas are buzzing with life, some are warm with mild use, others are quiet and cool.

Imagine a population density map of your identity. Throughout your mind, body, and soul is the life force of the nature of who you are. Some elements of your being are teeming with vitality, some are growing in maturity, and others have gone dormant (or never awoke to begin with).

The metaphor of a population density map helps us understand the "efficiencies" we display in each of the 27 expressions of the Enneagram. It highlights areas of low-occupation, mid-occupation, and high-occupation. A high score in 7w8 can be compared to a "high density" population in that region of your identity. A low score in 6w5 can be said to have a "low density" population. This means the numbers you score highest in are simply the regions of your identity you occupy most. The numbers that score in the mid-range are regions you occasionally visit, and low-scoring numbers represent regions you hardly ever encounter.

From a neurological perspective, this metaphor is accurate. The brain functions you have high familiarity with are more capable of creating increased efficiency, activation, and a higher volume of residency than regions that are unfamiliar to you or underutilized. This concept is clearly demonstrated in what is known as Hebbian Theory. **By increasing activity, you increase efficiency.** With this in mind, you can observe your individual population density map to expand your (w)holistic well-being.

BRAIN-BASED DIAGRAM

The **circle** of the Enneagram represents the global view of your whole identity. Within it are three distinct but united segments--instinct, intuition, and intellect. These **triads** represent the body, the soul, and the mind of a person, or the brain-stem, right hemisphere, and left hemisphere of the brain. Each of these Enneagram triads contain three unique **numbers** that represent three nuanced expressions of instinct, intuition, and intellect. These numbers are **symbols** for the expressions of our identity, and ultimately establish who we are.

(W)HOLISTIC IDENTITY DESCRIPTIONS

(Note: The end of the white paper provides a detailed definition of each of the following "(w)holistic definitions".)

Consciousness and Sub-Consciousness
Whole Enneagram Identity
Whole Human Being
Central Nervous System
Spiritual Well-being
Perichoresis and Kenosis
Divine Nature
Human/Divine Expressions
Behavior
Genetics and Epigenetics (Neuroplasticity)
Spiritual Practice
Emotional Expression
Processes and Pathways
Sense of Time
Communication Style
Performance Assessment Style
Perspective(s)
Self-Awareness
Survival-Based Responses
Law of Three

TRIAD DESCRIPTIONS

Below is a chart of the comparative language used to describe each of the three triads. This should give a fairly comprehensive overview of the characteristics each distinct triad represents.

Instinct	Intuition	Intellect
Gut Triad	Heart Triad	Head Triad
Body	Soul	Mind
Brain-stem	Right Brain	Left Brain
Physical Health	Emotional Health	Mental Health
8, 9, & 1 Integration	2, 3, & 4 Integration	5, 6, & 7 Integration
Son	Holy Spirit (Sophia)	Father
Reproductive	Feminine	Masculine
Action	Feelings	Thoughts
Nature	Nurture	Discipline
Stillness	Solitude	Silence
Primitive Emotions	Complex Expressed Emotions	Complex Control of Emotions
Practical Applications	Creative Focus	Analytical Focus
Past Tense	Present Tense	Future Tense
Unintentional Body Language	Intentional Body Language	Verbal Communication
Mechanics	Merit	Metric
Nano View	Macro View	Micro View
Moment-to-Moment, Second-by-Second	Month-to-Month, Year-to-Year	Hour-to-Hour, Day-to-Day
Fear & Impulsiveness	Attitude & Perspective	Caution & Attention
Reconciling	Affirming	Restraining

The diagram shows, globally,
who you are as a person.
Can you be a single number?
No. Not in isolation.

PART THREE

THE WHOLE-IDENTITY SCORING METHOD

A CASE STUDY

To effectively demonstrate how the Brain-Based Enneagram approach works, we will now walk through the Whole-Identity Profile scoring method utilizing a sample assessment.

*Please note the baseline scores reflected in this Whole-Identity Profile are provided by completing the RHETI assessment via the Enneagram Institute. This methodology can be applied to any Enneagram test that provides scores for all nine numbers.

WIP SCORING METHOD OVERVIEW

1. Take the RHETI test
2. Populate "Nature + Scores" list
3. Transcribe scores and calculate percentages for each of the 9 numbers on the diagram
4. Calculate scores and percentages for each triad on the diagram
5. Identify wing-relationships
6. Calculate scores and percentages for the "wing-relationships" list
7. Populate "Priorities/Motivations and Values" section
8. Populate "Travel Route(s)/Wing(s)" section
9. Populate "IVQ Results/Instincts" section

RHETI RESULTS

NATURE : SCORES

SURVIVAL STRATEGIES / UTILIZATION
EFFICIENCY RATING

Nature	Scores
2	24
6	19
3	18
7	18
9	16
1	14
4	13
8	13
5	9

DB/MPH HP/RPM

⊕ | USEFUL | SAFE
NEED: ° OF PRESENCE
"LIFE-GIVING"
↑ BUDGETED RESOURCES
↓ TAXES & INTEREST

⊜

↑ TAXES & INTEREST
↓ BUDGETED RESOURCES
"LIFE-THREATENING"
NEED: ° OF ABSENCE
⊖ | USELESS | UNSAFE

DB/MPH HP/RPM

DB: VOLUME, **HP**: STRENGTH,
MPH: SPEED, **RPM**: CAPACITY
⊕ GAS, ⊜ CRUISE, ⊖ BRAKE

POPULATION DENSITY MAP

ALL NINE NUMBERS = GLOBAL
TRIAD = CONTINENT
EACH NUMBER = A COUNTRY
WINGS = FLIGHT PLAN(S)

Numbers	Wing	Score	%
9, 1	9 w 1	30	= 10.42 %
1, 2	2 w 1	38	= 13.19 %
2, 3	2 w 3	42	= 14.58 %
3, 4	3 w 4	31	= 10.76 %
4, 5	4 w 5	22	= 7.64 %
5, 6	6 w 5	28	= 9.72 %
6, 7	7 w 6 / 6 w 7	37	= 12.85 %
7, 8	7 w 8	31	= 10.76 %
8, 9	9 w 8	29	= 10.07 %

100 % YOU

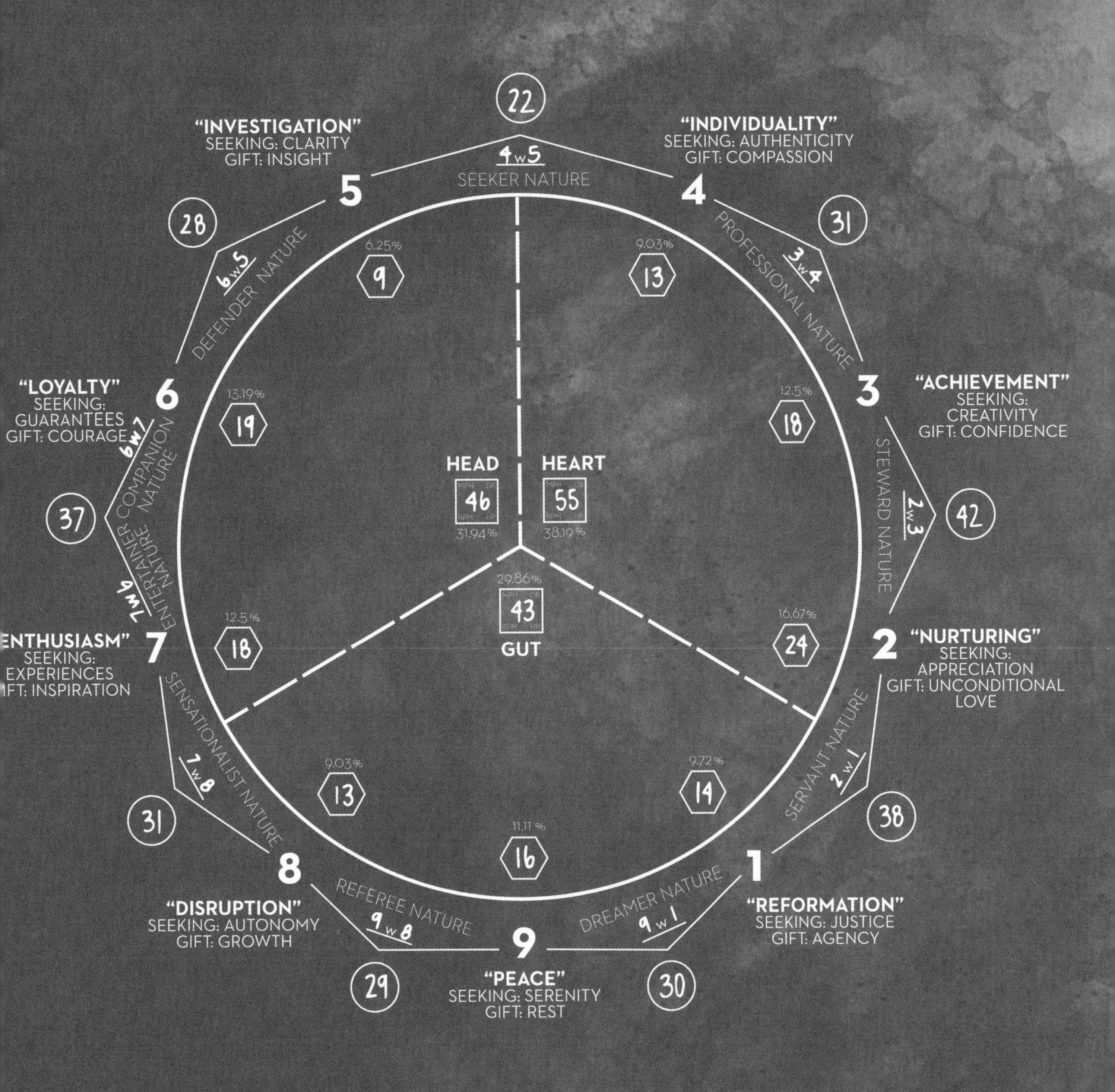

22
4w5
SEEKER NATURE
"INVESTIGATION"
SEEKING: CLARITY
GIFT: INSIGHT
5
"INDIVIDUALITY"
SEEKING: AUTHENTICITY
GIFT: COMPASSION
4
28
6w5
DEFENDER NATURE
31
3w4
PROFESSIONAL NATURE
6.25%
9
9.03%
13
"LOYALTY"
SEEKING:
GUARANTEES
GIFT: COURAGE
6
6w7
"ACHIEVEMENT"
SEEKING:
CREATIVITY
GIFT: CONFIDENCE
3
13.19%
19
12.5%
18
HEAD
46
31.94%
HEART
55
38.19%
COMPANION NATURE
37
ENTERTAINER NATURE
7w6
STEWARD NATURE
2w3
42
29.86%
43
GUT
"ENTHUSIASM"
SEEKING:
EXPERIENCES
GIFT: INSPIRATION
7
12.5%
18
16.67%
24
"NURTURING"
SEEKING:
APPRECIATION
GIFT: UNCONDITIONAL
LOVE
2
SENSATIONALIST NATURE
7w8
SERVANT NATURE
2w1
9.03%
13
9.72%
14
31
38
11.11%
16
8
"DISRUPTION"
SEEKING: AUTONOMY
GIFT: GROWTH
REFEREE NATURE
9w8
DREAMER NATURE
9w1
1
"REFORMATION"
SEEKING: JUSTICE
GIFT: AGENCY
9
"PEACE"
SEEKING: SERENITY
GIFT: REST
29
30

FILLING IN THE CIRCLE

Step 1 -- Take the RHETI Test

Step 2 -- Place your scores from highest to lowest on the right side of the "Nature + Scores" list. Then, write the corresponding Enneagram number to the left of each of the scores.

RHETI RESULTS

NATURE : SCORES

2 : 24
6 : 19

Step 3 -- Place your scores for each of the nine numbers in the hexagon beside each of the nine numbers, then divide each score by 144* to calculate the percentage of efficiency.

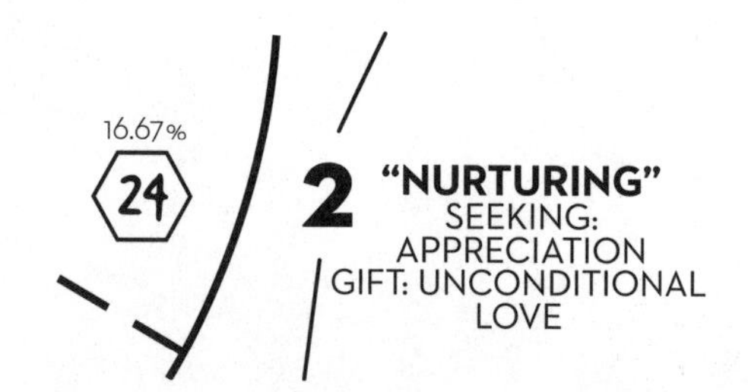

*Any number inside the global circle can be divided by 144 and any number outside of the circle can be divided by 288. Then take the resulting number and round to the 4th decimal point.
i.e. 32/288 = 11.11%, 17/144 = 11.80%.

Step 4 -- Combine the scores of the numbers that live within each triad (for heart add 2+3+4 together, for head add 5+6+7, and for gut add 8+9+1). Record the total scores of the corresponding triads in the squares located at the center of the diagram. Divide each of the three triad scores by 144 to calculate the percentage of efficiency in each.

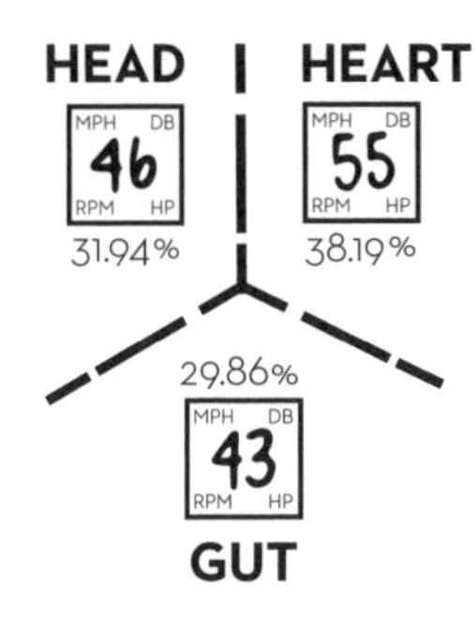

WING-RELATIONSHIPS (FLIGHT PLANS)

Step 5 -- For each of the nine numbers and their 18 wing expressions, you will likely have a preference toward one wing pair over the other. To identify your wings, review the scores for each pair of neighboring numbers. Between the two, identify the highest-scoring number. The high number is the central number and the low number is the wing. Record each of the highest-scoring wing pairs in the wing-relationships list in the bottom left corner.

For example, in the case study above, the score for number nine is 16 and the score for number one is 14. That means there is a higher efficiency in 9w1 than there is in 1w9. As another example, review the scores for 1 and 2. The score for number one is 14 and the score for number two is 24. That means there is a higher efficiency in 2w1 than there is in 1w2.

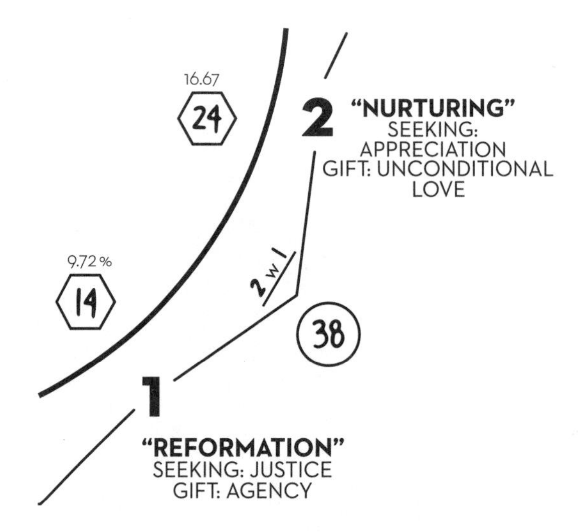

IF you have two scores in a wing relationship that are tied or within 1 point of each other, write down BOTH wing options, as we believe you can move in all 18 wings. Scores that are within one point offer easy movement back and forth between which number "sings lead' and which one "sings harmony". As such, record both options.

Step 6 -- To calculate the wing scores, add each neighboring pair of numbers together and place their combined score in the circles between them. For example, add the scores for numbers nine and one (16 + 14 = 30), and place that total in the circle between them. Then divide that number by 288 to calculate the percentage of efficiency (30/288 = .1042 = 10.42%). Record this information for each of the numbers in the wing-relationships list in the bottom left corner.

PRIORITIES/MOTIVATIONS/VALUES

Step 7 -- In the "Priorities/Motivations and Values" section, list each of your nine numbers in order from highest to lowest.

Step 8 -- In the "Travel Route(s)/Wing(s)" section, list your highest scoring wing relationships (any combined wing score of 35 or higher).

Step 9 -- In the "IVQ Results/Instincts" section, fill out the information you retrieved from your IVQ Results of your Sexual, Social and Self-preservation Instinct in the order received from the test.

*Please Note -- You can receive your IVQ results by taking the IVQ test via the Enneagram Institute (enneagraminstitute.com)

BRAIN-BASED DESCRIPTIONS

Once the diagram is populated, dig into your results.

BRAIN-BASED DESCRIPTIONS

INSTINCT
• GUT TRIAD
• BODY
• BRAIN-STEM
• PHYSICAL HEALTH
• 8, 9, & 1 INTEGRATION
• SON
• REPRODUCTIVE
• ACTION
• NATURE
• STILLNESS
• PRIMITIVE EMOTIONS
• PRACTICAL APPLICATIONS
• PAST TENSE
• UNINTENTIONAL BODY LANGUAGE
• MECHANICS
• NANO VIEW
• MOMENT-TO-MOMENT, SECOND-BY-SECOND
• FEAR & IMPULSIVENESS
• RECONCILING

8

DISRUPTION

The innate human capacity reflected in 8 nature is the energy of **Disruption**. What 8 nature seeks and is motivated by is **Autonomy**. Its primary style of engagement is **Action**. Positive limbic attachments reinforce a sense of being **In-control** and **Self-sufficient**. Negative limbic attachments are triggered fastest by **Dominance** or **Oppression**. When overwhelmed, fatigue expresses as **Panic**. The primary practical application for 8 nature is to breathe and practice **Stillness**.

Innate Gifting: The healthy 8 nature in each of us is the most gifted at modeling our human capacity for **Growth**.

8 wing 7 - Maverick nature

Central Value:
8 - Autonomy (*Subject*)
7 - Experiences (*Adjective*)
8w7 - Seeking to Experience Autonomy

Corresponding Brain Function:
8 - Brain-stem
7 - Left Hemisphere
8w7 - Driven by the brain-stem and left hemisphere

8 wing 9 - Bear nature

Central Value:
8 - Autonomy (*Subject*)
9 - Serenity (*Adjective*)
8w9 - Seeking Serene Autonomy

Corresponding Brain Function:
8 - Brain-stem
9 - Brain-stem
8w9 - Driven by the brain-stem

9

PEACE

The innate human capacity reflected in 9 nature is the energy of **Peace**. What 9 nature seeks and is motivated by is **Serenity**. Its primary style of engagement is **Action**. Positive limbic attachments reinforce a sense of being **Peaceful** and **Steady**. Negative limbic attachments are triggered fastest by **Conflict** or **Neglect**. When overwhelmed, fatigue expresses as **Panic**. The primary practical application for 9 nature is to breathe and practice **Stillness**.

Innate Gifting: The healthy 9 nature in each of us is the most gifted at modeling our human capacity for **Rest**.

9 wing 8 - Referee nature

Central Value:
9 - Serenity (*Subject*)
8 - Autonomy (*Adjective*)
9w8 - Seeking Autonomous Serenity

Corresponding Brain Function:
9 - Brain-stem
8 - Brain-stem
9w8 - Driven by the brain-stem

9 wing 1 - Dreamer nature

Central Value:
9 - Serenity (*Subject*)
1 - Justice (*Adjective*)
9w1 - Seeking Justified Serenity

Corresponding Brain Function:
9 - Brain-stem
1 - Brain-stem
9w1 - Driven by the brain-stem

1

REFORMATION

The innate human capacity reflected in 1 nature is the energy of **Reformation**. What 1 nature seeks and is motivated by is **Justice**. Its primary style of engagement is **Action**. Positive limbic attachments reinforce a sense of being **Right** and **Precise**. Negative limbic attachments are triggered fastest by **Injustice** or **Unfairness**. When overwhelmed, fatigue expresses as **Panic**. The primary practical application for 1 nature is to breathe and practice **Stillness**.

Innate Gifting: The healthy 1 nature in each of us is the most gifted at modeling our human capacity for **Agency**.

1 wing 9 - Idealist nature

Central Value:
1 - Justice (*Subject*)
9 - Serenity (*Adjective*)
1w9 - Seeking Serene Justice

Corresponding Brain Function:
1 - Brain-stem
9 - Brain-stem
1w9 - Driven by the brain-stem

1 wing 2 - Advocate nature

Central Value:
1 - Justice (*Subject*)
2 - Appreciation (*Adjective*)
1w2 - Seeking to Appreciate Justice

Corresponding Brain Function:
1 - Brain-stem
2 - Right Hemisphere
1w2 - Driven by the brain-stem and the right hemisphere

NURTURING

The innate human capacity reflected in 2 nature is the energy of **Nurturing**. What 2 nature seeks and is motivated by is **Appreciation**. Its primary style of engagement is **Emotion**. Positive limbic attachments reinforce a sense of being **Valuable** and **Worthy**. Negative limbic attachments are triggered fastest by **Criticism** or **Disrespect**. When overwhelmed, fatigue expresses as **Depression**. The primary practical application for 2 nature is to breathe and practice **Solitude**.

Innate Gifting: The healthy 2 nature in each of us is the most gifted at modeling our human capacity for **Unconditional Love**.

2 wing 1 - Servant nature

Central Value:
2 - Appreciation (*Subject*)
1 - Justice (*Adjective*)
2w1 - Seeking Justified Appreciation

Corresponding Brain Function:
2 - Right Hemisphere
1 - Brain-stem
2w1 - Driven by the right hemisphere and the brain-stem

2 wing 3 - Steward nature

Central Value:
2 - Appreciation (*Subject*)
3 - Creativity (*Adjective*)
2w3 - Seeking to Create Appreciation

Corresponding Brain Function:
2 - Right Hemisphere
3 - Right Hemisphere
2w3 - Driven by the right hemisphere

INTUITION
• HEART TRIAD
• SOUL
• RIGHT BRAIN
• EMOTIONAL HEALTH
• 2, 3, & 4 INTEGRATION
• HOLY SPIRIT (SOPHIA)
• FEMININE
• FEELINGS
• NURTURE
• SOLITUDE
• COMPLEX EXPRESSED EMOTIONS
• CREATIVE FOCUS
• PRESENT TENSE
• INTENTIONAL BODY LANGUAGE
• MERIT
• MACRO VIEW
• MONTH-TO-MONTH, YEAR-TO-YEAR
• ATTITUDE & PERSPECTIVE
• AFFIRMING

3

ACHIEVEMENT

The innate human capacity reflected in 3 nature is the energy of **Achievement**. What 3 nature seeks and is motivated by is **Creativity**. Its primary style of engagement is **Emotion**. Positive limbic attachments reinforce a sense of being **Effective** and **Successful**. Negative limbic attachments are triggered fastest by **Failure** or **Inadequacy**. When overwhelmed, fatigue expresses as **Depression**. The primary practical application for 3 nature is to breathe and practice **Solitude**.

Innate Gifting: The healthy 3 nature in each of us is the most gifted at modeling our human capacity for **Confidence**.

3 wing 2 - Charmer nature

Central Value:
3 - Creativity (*Subject*)
2 - Appreciation (*Adjective*)
3w2 - Seeking to Appreciate Creativity

Corresponding Brain Function:
3 - Right Hemisphere
2 - Right Hemisphere
3w2 - Driven by the right hemisphere

3 wing 4 - Professional nature

Central Value:
3 - Creativity (*Subject*)
4 - Authenticity (*Adjective*)
3w4 - Seeking Authentic Creativity

Corresponding Brain Function:
3 - Right Hemisphere
4 - Right Hemisphere
3w4 - Driven by the right hemisphere

4

INDIVIDUALITY

The innate human capacity reflected in 4 nature is the energy of **Individuality**. What 4 nature seeks and is motivated by is **Authenticity**. Its primary style of engagement is **Emotion**. Positive limbic attachments reinforce a sense of being **Truthful** and **Deep**. Negative limbic attachments are triggered fastest by **Dishonesty** or **Superficiality**. When overwhelmed, fatigue expresses as **Depression**. The primary practical application for 4 nature is to breathe and practice **Solitude**.

Innate Gifting: The healthy 4 nature in each of us is the most gifted at modeling our human capacity for **Compassion**.

4 wing 3 - Influencer nature

Central Value:
4 - Authenticity (*Subject*)
3 - Creativity (*Adjective*)
4w3 - Seeking to Create Authenticity

Corresponding Brain Function:
4 - Right Hemisphere
3 - Right Hemisphere
4w3 - Driven by the right hemisphere

4 wing 5 - Seeker nature

Central Value:
4 - Authenticity (*Subject*)
5 - Clarity (*Adjective*)
4w5 - Seeking Clear Authenticity

Corresponding Brain Function:
4 - Right Hemisphere
5 - Left Hemisphere
4w5 - Driven by the right and left hemispheres

INTELLECT
• HEAD TRIAD
• MIND
• LEFT BRAIN
• MENTAL HEALTH
• 5, 6, & 7 INTEGRATION
• FATHER
• MASCULINE
• THOUGHTS
• DISCIPLINE
• SILENCE
• COMPLEX CONTROL OF EMOTIONS
• ANALYTICAL FOCUS
• FUTURE TENSE
• VERBAL COMMUNICATION
• METRIC
• MICRO VIEW
• HOUR-TO-HOUR, DAY-TO-DAY
• CAUTION & ATTENTION
• RESTRAINING

5

INVESTIGATION

The innate human capacity reflected in 5 nature is the energy of **Investigation**. What 5 nature seeks and is motivated by is **Clarity**. Its primary style of engagement is **Thought**. Positive limbic attachments reinforce a sense of being **Accurate** and **Lucid**. Negative limbic attachments are triggered fastest by **Ambiguity** and **Incompetence**. When overwhelmed, fatigue expresses as **Anxiety**. The primary practical application for 5 nature is to breathe and practice **Silence**.

Innate Gifting: The healthy 5 nature in each of us is the most gifted at modeling our human capacity for **Insight**.

5 wing 4 - Innovator nature

Central Value:
5 - Clarity (*Subject*)
4 - Authenticity (*Adjective*)
5w4 - Seeking Authentic Clarity

Corresponding Brain Function:
5 - Left Hemisphere
4 - Right Hemisphere
5w4 - **Driven by the left and right hemispheres**

5 wing 6 - Problem-Solver nature

Central Value:
5 - Clarity (*Subject*)
6 - Guarantees (*Adjective*)
5w6 - Seeking Guaranteed Clarity

Corresponding Brain Function:
5 - Left Hemisphere
6 - Left Hemisphere
5w6 - **Driven by the left hemisphere**

6

LOYALTY

The innate human capacity reflected in 6 nature is the energy of **Loyalty**. What 6 nature seeks and is motivated by is **Guarantees**. Its primary style of engagement is **Thought**. Positive limbic attachments reinforce a sense of being **Concrete** and **Promised**. Negative limbic attachments are triggered fastest by **Unpredictability** or **Insecurity**. When overwhelmed, fatigue expresses as **Anxiety**. The primary practical application for 6 nature is to breathe and practice **Silence**.

Innate Gifting: The healthy 6 nature in each of us is the most gifted at modeling our human capacity for **Courage**.

6 wing 5 - Defender nature

Central Value:
6 - Guarantees (*Subject*)
5 - Clarity (*Adjective*)
6w5 - **Seeking Clarified Guarantees**

Corresponding Brain Function:
6 - Left Hemisphere
5 - Left Hemisphere
6w5 - **Driven by the left hemisphere**

6 wing 7 - Companion nature

Central Value:
6 - Guarantees (*Subject*)
7 - Experiences (*Adjective*)
6w7 - **Seeking to Experience Guarantees**

Corresponding Brain Function:
6 - Left Hemisphere
7 - Left Hemisphere
6w7 - **Driven by the left hemisphere**

7

ENTHUSIASM

The innate human capacity reflected in 7 nature is the energy of **Enthusiasm**. What 7 nature seeks and is motivated by are **Experiences**. Its primary style of engagement is **Thought**. Positive limbic attachments reinforce a sense of being **Adventurous** and **Sensational**. Negative limbic attachments are triggered fastest by **Inaction** or **Monotony**. When overwhelmed, fatigue expresses as **Anxiety**. The primary practical application for 7 nature is to breathe and practice **Silence**.

Innate Gifting: The healthy 7 nature in each of us is the most gifted at modeling our human capacity for **Inspiration**.

7 wing 6 - Entertainer nature

Central Value:
7 - Experiences (*Subject*)
6 - Guarantees (*Adjective*)
7w6 - **Seeking Guaranteed Experiences**

Corresponding Brain Function:
7 - Left Hemisphere
6 - Left Hemisphere
7w6 - **Driven by the left hemisphere**

7 wing 8 - Sensationalist nature

Central Value:
7 - Experiences (*Subject*)
8 - Autonomy (*Adjective*)
7w8 - **Seeking Autonomous Experiences**

Corresponding Brain Function:
7 - Left Hemisphere
8 - Brain-stem
7w8 - **Driven by the left hemisphere and the brain-stem**

We can connect with and express the innate capacity, energy, essence, and motivations of each number when we approach the relational nature of the whole.

PART FOUR

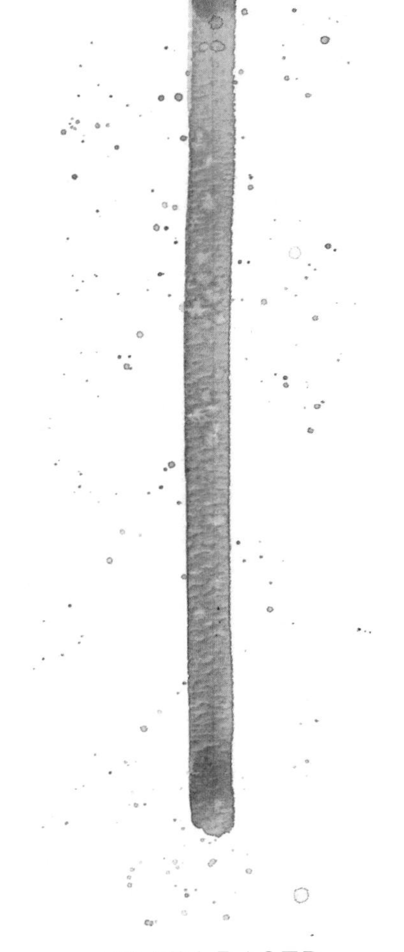

BRAIN-BASED PRACTICAL APPLICATIONS

> "Learning is physical.
> Learning means the modification, growth, and pruning of our neurons and synapses. Through experience, we are cultivating our own neuronal networks."
>
> *- Dr. James Zull, Professor of Biology and Biochemistry at Case Western University*

GROWTH FOR ALL NINE NUMBERS

The most exciting implications of the Brain-Based Enneagram are the practical ones because those are the ones that instigate real change. New theory is only helpful when it is accessible and actionable, so in this section we apply the (w)holistic model of the Brain-Based Enneagram to our lives, bearing in mind that this is only the high-level view and there is much to be expanded upon.

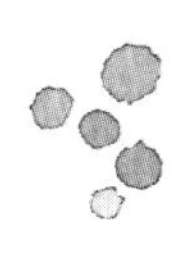

Two things matter here: (1) The health of each individual number and (2) The health of the relationships between them. As you engage with the practical applications below, keep in mind that the goal is not to improve each number in isolation, but to improve them in relationship. Remember, you are not a personality. You have an identity, and the health of your identity depends upon the way each of the nine numbers intersect and relate with the whole of who you are.

To properly utilize the Brain-Based Enneagram, you must maintain a global view. The circular diagram is helpful in this way. Imagine the circle as a whole, integrated representation of who you are, and each of the nine numbers as parts to the whole of your identity. Growth is optimized when the goal is aimed towards rounding out the whole of who you are, rather than skyrocketing the isolated improvement of any single expression.

THESAURUS EXERCISE

Language is a powerful tool for understanding and connecting new ideas--it isn't meant to become a barrier to entry. If any word in this process causes distraction or triggers you negatively, choose a more helpful word. We each have experiences--positive, neutral, negative--that shape our language and trigger associations with the words we use. The goal is to craft a relevant vocabulary that encourages engagement, safety, and understanding as you journey through your personal identification with the Brain-Based Enneagram. Here we offer a process for building custom Enneagram language for optimal growth.

Optimize Your Language

1. Using an online thesaurus, type the nature-word of each number into the search bar.

NATURE WORDS:
8 -- Disrupt
9 -- Peace
1 -- Reform
2 -- Nurture
3 -- Achieve
4 -- Individuality
5 -- Investigate
6 -- Loyalty
7 -- Enthusiasm

2. Once you've typed the first word, hit search. When the list populates with synonyms, notice how many of the words feel unsafe, and how many feel safe. Click the word that feels safest or most enjoyable to you.

3. When the list populates again, click the word that feels safest or most enjoyable to you.

4. When the list populates again, click the word that feels safest or most enjoyable to you.

5. Review the list. If all or most of the words feel safe and enjoyable to you, you're done! The word at the top of the page, because it carries positive associations, can be integrated or substituted into your personal Enneagram vocabulary instead of (or in addition to) the original "nature" word for this number.

For example, search “Disrupt”

If the list feels primarily unsafe, select the safest, most enjoyable relevant word. Perhaps “Shake”.

If the list is still largely unsafe, select the safest, most enjoyable relevant word. Perhaps “Move”.

If the list still feels primarily unsafe, select the safest, most enjoyable relevant word. Perhaps “Advance”.

Results: “Advance” can stand in place of “Disrupt”. Without changing the nature of the number, you can eliminate trigger words and create language that invites positive engagement.

6. Repeat this process for each number until you have a lexicon of positive terms. Feel free to use this exercise for *any* word in this document that stimulates a negative response.

*Caveat: Be sure to follow a trail of *relevant* words. For example, you wouldn't click “Disrupt → Shake → Twitter → Teehee” since “Teehee” isn't likely going to be a helpful substitute for “Disrupt”. Instead, select the safest *most relevant* words. For even better results, select words that are *personally relevant* to you as well. Identify and select the words that evoke strong positive responses, or are connected in a personal way to your lived experience. If necessary, click through the tabs at the top of the lists to select the word bank that most closely resembles the *nature* of the original word.

SWOT ANALYSIS

A SWOT analysis measures and gives suggestions for (S) how to promote your strengths, (W) how to improve your weaknesses, (O) how to exercise your opportunities, and (T) how to mitigate threats. Here we offer positive, pragmatic and engaging suggestions for optimal growth for each number.

8 ACTION STEPS (BODY)

Innate Human Nature: **Disrupt**
Innate Human Motivation: **Autonomy**
Innate Gifting: **Growth**

S

Promote Strengths (Leverage Your Gifts)

You are naturally efficient in utilizing the **Instinctual** Intelligence center. Powerful exercises for increasing Whole-Brain health via **Brain-stem activation** include:

Meditate with the specific intention of embodiment (body scanning, somatic experiencing, focused movement, etc)

Engage in weight-bearing, fine-motor, body-based exercises such as: Tai Chi, Yoga, Qi Gong, Jiu Jitsu, etc

Practice focused 4-7-8 breath work (as you breathe, count to 4, hold for 7, breathe out for 8)

Walk 15-17,000 steps per day (Begin with 1K and increase as your body allows)

W

Improve Weaknesses (Strategies for Stamina and Strength)

Prioritize Emotional Intelligence and Mental Health

Thesaurus Exercise: Build a lexicon of positive, pragmatic and/or engaging words for the 'nature', 'motivation', and 'gifting' of this number (left) using the Thesaurus Exercise Instructions (pp. 66-68).

O

Exercise Opportunities (Activate Your Brain)

Brain-stem (natural activation)
What positive actions can you take in response to the autonomy you experience?

Right Brain (intentional activation)
What does a healthy emotional relationship with autonomy mean to you?

Left Brain (intentional activation)
Examine specific moments where you encountered life-giving autonomy today. How can you pragmatically encourage more experiences like this?

T

Mitigate Threats (There are no bears)

When you are overwhelmed, fatigue often expresses as panic. Consider:

How do you respond when your sense of control and self-sufficiency are threatened?

Is this reaction appropriate?
Are you aware of your breath?

Consider your response when dominance and oppression are present

Is this reaction appropriate?
Are you aware of your breath?

Practice stillness internally (possibly with or without others) and engage in breath awareness

9 ACTION STEPS (BODY)

Innate Human Nature: **Peace**
Innate Human Motivation: **Serenity**
Innate Gifting: **Rest**

S

Promote Strengths
(Leverage Your Gifts)

You are naturally efficient in utilizing the **Instinctual** Intelligence center. Powerful exercises for increasing Whole-Brain health via **Brain-stem activation** include:

Meditate with the specific intention of embodiment (body scanning, somatic experiencing, focused movement, etc)

Engage in weight-bearing, fine-motor, body-based exercises such as: Tai Chi, Yoga, Qi Gong, Jiu Jitsu, etc

Practice focused 4-7-8 breath work (as you breathe, count to 4, hold for 7, breathe out for 8)

Walk 15-17,000 steps per day (Begin with 1K and increase as your body allows)

W

Improve Weaknesses
(Strategies for Stamina and Strength)

Prioritize Emotional Intelligence and Mental Health

Thesaurus Exercise: Build a lexicon of positive, pragmatic and/or engaging words for the 'nature', 'motivation', and 'gifting' of this number (left) using the Thesaurus Exercise Instructions (pp. 66-68).

O

Exercise Opportunities (Activate Your Brain)

Brain-stem (natural activation)
What positive actions can you take in response to the serenity you experience?

Right Brain (intentional activation)
What does a healthy emotional relationship with serenity mean to you?

Left Brain (intentional activation)
Examine specific moments where you encountered life-giving serenity today. How can you pragmatically encourage more experiences like this?

T

Mitigate Threats (There are no bears)

When you are overwhelmed, fatigue often expresses as panic. Consider:

How do you respond when your sense of peace and steadiness are threatened?

Is this reaction appropriate?
Are you aware of your breath?

Consider your response when conflict and neglect are present

Is this reaction appropriate?
Are you aware of your breath?

Practice stillness externally (possibly with others) and engage in breath awareness

1 ACTION STEPS (BODY)

Innate Human Nature: **Reform**
Innate Human Motivation: **Justice**
Innate Gifting: **Agency**

S

Promote Strengths (Leverage Your Gifts)

You are naturally efficient in utilizing the **Instinctual** Intelligence center. Powerful exercises for increasing Whole-Brain health via **Brain-stem activation** include:

Meditate with the specific intention of embodiment (body scanning, somatic experiencing, focused movement, etc)

Engage in weight-bearing, fine-motor, body-based exercises such as: Tai Chi, Yoga, Qi Gong, Jiu Jitsu, etc

Practice focused 4-7-8 breath work (as you breathe, count to 4, hold for 7, breathe out for 8)

Walk 15-17,000 steps per day (Begin with 1K and increase as your body allows)

W

Improve Weaknesses (Strategies for Stamina and Strength)

Prioritize Emotional Intelligence and Mental Health

Thesaurus Exercise: Build a lexicon of positive, pragmatic and/or engaging words for the 'nature', 'motivation', and 'gifting' of this number (left) using the Thesaurus Exercise Instructions (pp. 66-68).

O

Exercise Opportunities
(Activate Your Brain)

Brain-stem (natural activation)
What positive actions can you take in response to the justice you experience?

Right Brain (intentional activation)
What does a healthy emotional relationship with justice mean to you?

Left Brain (intentional activation)
Examine specific moments where you encountered life-giving justice today. How can you pragmatically encourage more experiences like this?

T

Mitigate Threats
(There are no bears)

When you are overwhelmed, fatigue often expresses as panic. Consider:

How do you respond when your sense of rightness and precision are threatened?

Is this reaction appropriate?
Are you aware of your breath?

Consider your response when injustice and unfairness are present

Is this reaction appropriate?
Are you aware of your breath?

Practice stillness internally (possibly without others) and engage in breath awareness

2 ACTION STEPS (HEART)

Innate Human Nature: **Nurture**
Innate Human Motivation: **Appreciation**
Innate Gifting: **Unconditional Love**

S

Promote Strengths (Leverage Your Gifts)

You are naturally efficient in utilizing the **Intuitive** Intelligence center. Powerful exercises for increasing Whole-Brain health via **Right Brain activation** include:

Meditate with no specific intention (centering prayer, interior silence, self-emptying meditation, etc)

Engage with art/abstract journaling

Practice focused 4-7-8 breath work (as you breathe, count to 4, hold for 7, breathe out for 8)

Exercise self-awareness by increasing your emotional literacy (articulate, identify, and name your emotions). See Brené Brown's 30 Core Emotions

W

Improve Weaknesses (Strategies for Stamina and Strength)

Cultivate Physical and Mental Health

Thesaurus Exercise: Build a lexicon of positive, pragmatic and/or engaging words for the 'nature', 'motivation', and 'gifting' of this number (left) using the Thesaurus Exercise Instructions (pp. 66-68).

O

Exercise Opportunities (Activate Your Brain)

Right Brain (natural activation)
What does a healthy emotional relationship with appreciation look like for you?

Brain-stem (intentional activation)
What positive actions can you take in response to the appreciation you experience?

Left Brain (intentional activation)
Examine specific moments where you encountered life-giving appreciation today. How can you pragmatically encourage more experiences like this?

T

Mitigate Threats (There are no bears)

When you are overwhelmed, fatigue often expresses as depression. Consider:

How do you respond when your sense of value and worthiness are threatened?

Is this reaction appropriate?
Are you aware of your breath?

Consider your response when criticism and disrespect are present

Is this reaction appropriate?
Are you aware of your breath?

Practice solitude internally (possibly without others) and engage in breath awareness

3 ACTION STEPS (HEART)

Innate Human Nature: **Achievement**
Innate Human Motivation: **Creativity**
Innate Gifting: **Confidence**

S

Promote Strengths
(Leverage Your Gifts)

You are naturally efficient in utilizing the **Intuitive** Intelligence center. Powerful exercises for increasing Whole-Brain health via **Right Brain activation** include:

Meditate with no specific intention (centering prayer, interior silence, self-emptying meditation, etc)

Engage with art/abstract journaling

Practice focused 4-7-8 breath work (as you breathe, count to 4, hold for 7, breathe out for 8)

Exercise self-awareness by increasing your emotional literacy (articulate, identify, and name your emotions). See Brené Brown's 30 Core Emotions

W

Improve Weaknesses
(Strategies for Stamina and Strength)

Cultivate Physical and Mental Health

Thesaurus Exercise: Build a lexicon of positive, pragmatic and/or engaging words for the 'nature', 'motivation', and 'gifting' of this number (left) using the Thesaurus Exercise Instructions (pp. 66-68).

O

Exercise Opportunities
(Activate Your Brain)

Right Brain (natural activation)
What does a healthy emotional relationship with creativity look like for you?

Brain-stem (intentional activation)
What positive actions can you take in response to the creativity you experience?

Left Brain (intentional activation)
Examine specific moments where you encountered life-giving creativity today. How can you pragmatically encourage more experiences like this?

T

Mitigate Threats
(There are no bears)

When you are overwhelmed, fatigue often expresses as depression. Consider:

How do you respond when your sense of effectiveness and success are threatened?

Is this reaction appropriate?
Are you aware of your breath?

Consider your response when failure and inadequacy are present.

Is this reaction appropriate?
Are you aware of your breath?

Practice solitude internally (possibly with or without others) and engage in breath awareness

4 ACTION STEPS (HEART)

Innate Human Nature: **Individuality**
Innate Human Motivation: **Authenticity**
Innate Gifting: **Compassion**

S

Promote Strengths
(Leverage Your Gifts)

You are naturally efficient in utilizing the **Intuitive** Intelligence center. Powerful exercises for increasing Whole-Brain health via **Right Brain activation** include:

Meditate with no specific intention (centering prayer, interior silence, self-emptying meditation, etc)

Engage with art/abstract journaling

Practice focused 4-7-8 breath work (as you breathe, count to 4, hold for 7, breathe out for 8)

Exercise self-awareness by increasing your emotional literacy (articulate, identify, and name your emotions). See Brené Brown's 30 Core Emotions

W

Improve Weaknesses
(Strategies for Stamina and Strength)

Cultivate Physical and Mental Health

Thesaurus Exercise: Build a lexicon of positive, pragmatic and/or engaging words for the 'nature', 'motivation', and 'gifting' of this number (left) using the Thesaurus Exercise Instructions (pp. 66-68).

O

Exercise Opportunities (Activate Your Brain)

Right Brain (natural activation)
What does a healthy emotional relationship with authenticity look like for you?

Brain-stem (intentional activation)
What positive actions can you take in response to the authenticity you experience?

Left Brain (intentional activation)
Examine specific moments where you encountered life-giving authenticity today. How can you pragmatically encourage more experiences like this?

T

Mitigate Threats (There are no bears)

When you are overwhelmed, fatigue often expresses as depression. Consider:

How do you respond when your sense of truth and depth are threatened?

Is this reaction appropriate?
Are you aware of your breath?

Consider your response when dishonesty and superficiality are present

Is this reaction appropriate?
Are you aware of your breath?

Practice solitude externally (possibly with others) and engage in breath awareness

5 ACTION STEPS (HEAD)

Innate Human Nature: **Investigate**
Innate Human Motivation: **Clarity**
Innate Gifting: **Insight**

S

Promote Strengths
(Leverage Your Gifts)

You are naturally efficient in utilizing the **Intellectual** Intelligence center. Powerful exercises for increasing Whole-Brain health via **Left Brain activation** include:

Meditate with a specific intention in mind (desired action steps, a sacred word, positive affirmations, etc)

Engage with stream-of-conscious journaling

Practice focused 4-7-8 breath work (as you breathe, count to 4, hold for 7, breathe out for 8)

Task out using the Pomodoro Technique (25 minutes of focused work, 5 minute break, repeat)

W

Improve Weaknesses
(Strategies for Stamina and Strength)

Develop your Emotional Intelligence and Physical Health

Thesaurus Exercise: Build a lexicon of positive, pragmatic and/or engaging words for the 'nature', 'motivation', and 'gifting' of this number (left) using the Thesaurus Exercise Instructions (pp. 66-68).

O

Exercise Opportunities
(Activate Your Brain)

Left Brain (natural activation)
Examine specific moments where you encountered life-giving clarity today. How can you pragmatically encourage more experiences like this?

Right Brain (intentional activation)
What does a healthy emotional relationship with clarity look like for you?

Brain-stem (intentional activation)
What positive actions can you take in response to the clarity you experience?

T

Mitigate Threats
(There are no bears)

When you are overwhelmed, fatigue often expresses as anxiety. Consider:

How do you respond when your sense of accuracy and lucidity are threatened?

Is this reaction appropriate?
Are you aware of your breath?

Consider your response when ambiguity and incompetence are present

Is this reaction appropriate?
Are you aware of your breath?

Practice silence externally (possibly with others) and engage in breath awareness

6 ACTION STEPS (HEAD)

Innate Human Nature: **Loyalty**
Innate Human Motivation: **Guarantees**
Innate Gifting: **Courage**

S

Promote Strengths
(Leverage Your Gifts)

You are naturally efficient in utilizing the **Intellectual** Intelligence center. Powerful exercises for increasing Whole-Brain health via **Left Brain activation** include:

Meditate with a specific intention in mind (desired action steps, a sacred word, positive affirmations, etc)

Engage with stream-of-conscious journaling

Practice focused 4-7-8 breath work (as you breathe, count to 4, hold for 7, breathe out for 8)

Task out using the Pomodoro Technique (25 minutes of focused work, 5 minute break, repeat)

W

Improve Weaknesses
(Strategies for Stamina and Strength)

Develop your Emotional Intelligence and Physical Health

Thesaurus Exercise: Build a lexicon of positive, pragmatic and/or engaging words for the 'nature', 'motivation', and 'gifting' of this number (left) using the Thesaurus Exercise Instructions (pp. 66-68).

O

Exercise Opportunities
(Activate Your Brain)

Left Brain (natural activation)
Examine specific moments where you encountered life-giving guarantees today. How can you pragmatically encourage more experiences like this?

Right Brain (intentional activation)
What does a healthy emotional relationship with guarantees look like for you?

Brain-stem (intentional activation)
What positive actions can you take in response to the guarantees you experience?

T

Mitigate Threats
(There are no bears)

When you are overwhelmed, fatigue often expresses as anxiety. Consider:

How do you respond when your sense of concreteness and certainty are threatened?

Is this reaction appropriate?
Are you aware of your breath?

Consider your response when unpredictability and insecurity are present

Is this reaction appropriate?
Are you aware of your breath?

Practice silence internally (possibly with or without others) and engage in breath awareness

7 ACTION STEPS (HEAD)

Innate Human Nature: **Enthusiasm**
Innate Human Motivation: **Experiences**
Innate Gifting: **Inspiration**

S

Promote Strengths (Leverage Your Gifts)

You are naturally efficient in utilizing the **Intellectual** Intelligence center. Powerful exercises for increasing Whole-Brain health via **Left Brain activation** include:

Meditate with a specific intention in mind (desired action steps, a sacred word, positive affirmations, etc)

Engage with stream-of-conscious journaling

Practice focused 4-7-8 breath work (as you breathe, count to 4, hold for 7, breathe out for 8)

Task out using the Pomodoro Technique (25 minutes of focused work, 5 minute break, repeat)

W

Improve Weaknesses (Strategies for Stamina and Strength)

Develop your Emotional Intelligence and Physical Health

Thesaurus Exercise: Build a lexicon of positive, pragmatic and/or engaging words for the 'nature', 'motivation', and 'gifting' of this number (left) using the Thesaurus Exercise Instructions (pp. 66-68).

O

Exercise Opportunities (Activate Your Brain)

Left Brain (natural activation)

Examine specific moments where you encountered life-giving experiences today. How can you pragmatically encourage more experiences like this?

Right Brain (intentional activation)

What does a healthy emotional relationship with experiences look like for you?

Brain-stem (intentional activation)

What positive actions can you take in response to the experiences you encountered?

T

Mitigate Threats (There are no bears)

When you are overwhelmed, fatigue often expresses as anxiety. Consider:

How do you respond when your sense of adventure and sensations are threatened?

Is this reaction appropriate?
Are you aware of your breath?

Consider your response when inaction and monotony are present

Is this reaction appropriate?
Are you aware of your breath?

Practice silence internally internally (possibly without others) and engage in breath awareness

Practice doesn't
make perfect.
It makes
permanent.

PART FIVE

WHOLE-IDENTITY, WHOLE HUMAN

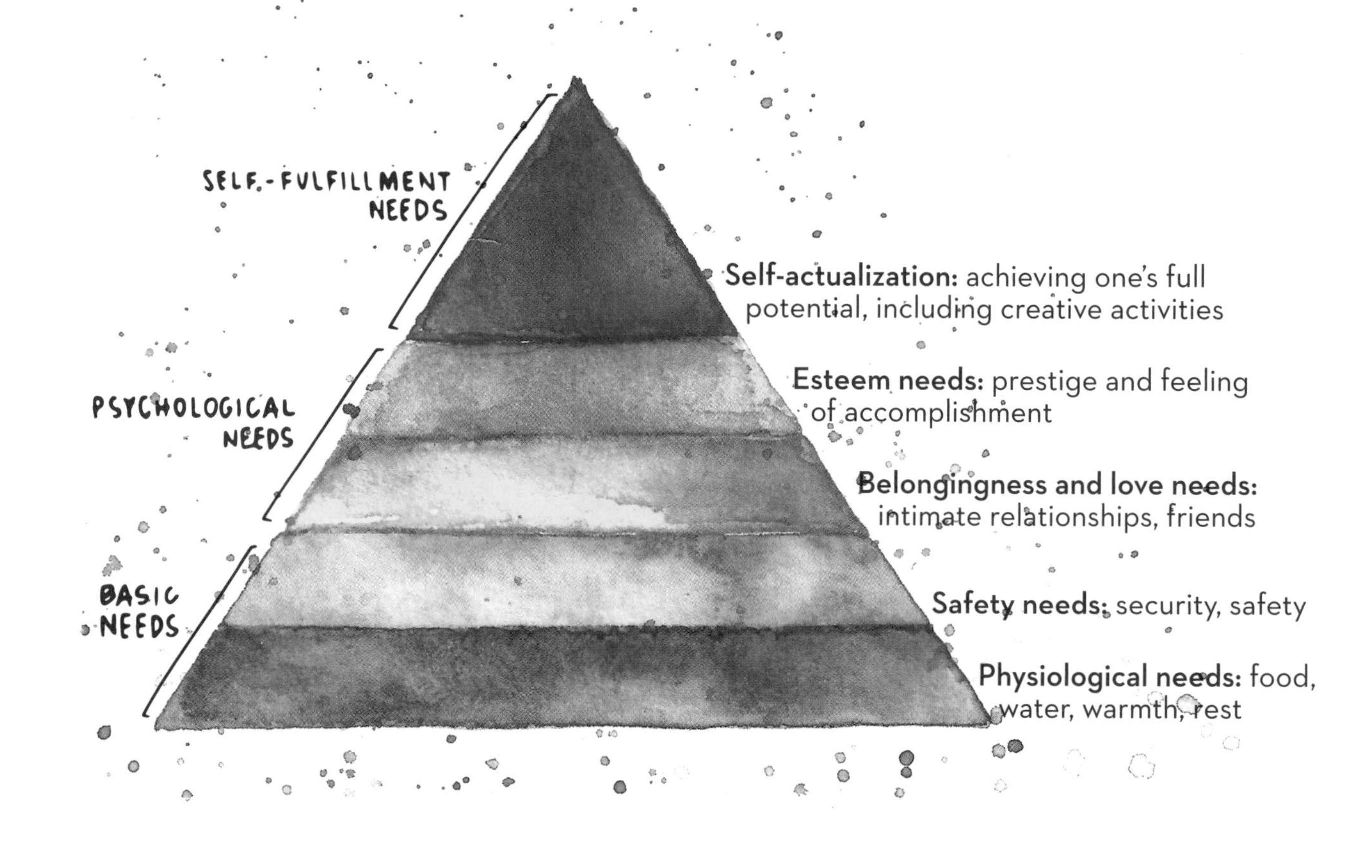
SELF-FULFILLMENT NEEDS
PSYCHOLOGICAL NEEDS
BASIC NEEDS
Self-actualization: achieving one's full potential, including creative activities
Esteem needs: prestige and feeling of accomplishment
Belongingness and love needs: intimate relationships, friends
Safety needs: security, safety
Physiological needs: food, water, warmth, rest

The Brain-Based Enneagram is not about being less broken, it is about becoming more whole.

THE CYCLE OF SELF-ACTUALIZATION

When faced with the overwhelming idea of where to begin, Maslow's Hierarchy is a helpful tool for understanding the priorities of self-care and personal well-being.

To grow, start at the bottom. Your basic needs must first be met in order to create a safe environment for sustained improvement. If your need for water and sleep is extreme, your desire for creative activity can (and should) be placed on the backburner. In contrast, if you are satisfied in your intimate relationships and friendships, capacity for achieving your full potential is more likely to be available to you, and you are safe to pursue it. You can use this information to influence the way you engage with the Brain-Based applications for growth.

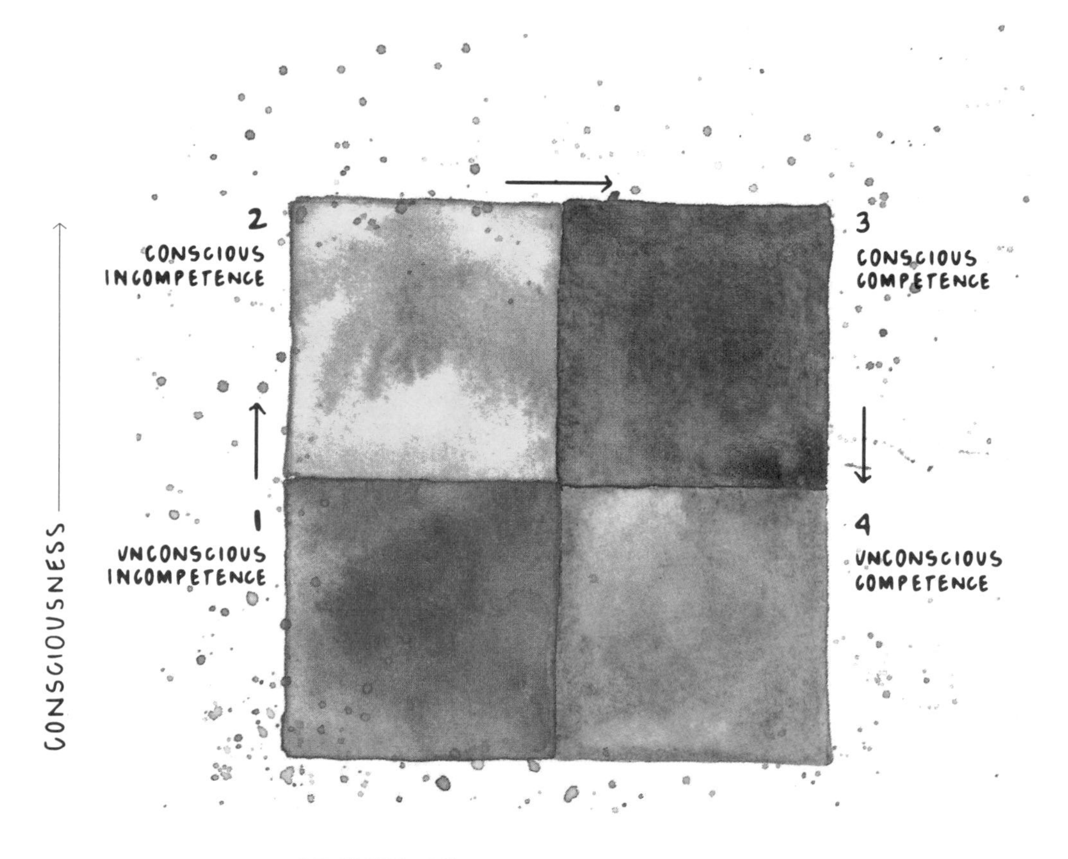
2
CONSCIOUS
INCOMPETENCE
3
CONSCIOUS
COMPETENCE
1
UNCONSCIOUS
INCOMPETENCE
4
UNCONSCIOUS
COMPETENCE
CONSCIOUSNESS
COMPETENCE

The essential principle to bear in mind when utilizing Maslow's Hierarchy for self-actualization is that the process of self-actualization itself is not linear. It is fractal. Throughout your lifetime, you will experience the hierarchy again and again as you engage and re-engage with the integrated nature of your evolving identity. As you progress through each phase of growth, you become more competent and efficient in each distinct expression of your identity. This is how maturity develops.

For a helpful model of the cyclical nature of growth, we can turn to The Four Stages of Competence theory. The Brain-Based Enneagram relies on this process: Unconscious Incompetence → Conscious Incompetence → Conscious Competence → Unconscious Competence.

Unconscious Incompetence
You don't know what you don't know
Conscious Incompetence
You know what you don't know
Conscious Competence
You know what you know
Unconscious Competence
You don't know what you know,
but you know it anyway

The goal of the Brain-Based Enneagram is to provide tools that create awareness and integrate healthy patterns and behaviors so effectively into your identity that they become second nature to you (unconscious competence), empowering you to access their expressions subconsciously and with ease. For as long as you are alive, you are never done transforming. The Brain-Based Enneagram is a life-long tool built for continued (w)holistic improvement.

WHOLE-IDENTITY DESCRIPTIONS

Below is a glossary of 20 high-level terms and descriptions of how a Whole-Identity perspective impacts (w)holistic well-being and growth.

CONSCIOUSNESS & SUB-CONSCIOUSNESS	I am instinctive, intuitive, and intellectual. I experience a varying degree of both conscious and subconscious interactions collectively and simultaneously.
WHOLE ENNEAGRAM IDENTITY	I am a whole identity. I experience all three intelligence centers (head, heart, and gut) collectively and simultaneously.
WHOLE HUMAN BEING	I am a whole human being. I experience the world via my mind, body, and soul collectively and simultaneously.
CENTRAL NERVOUS SYSTEM	I have a complete central nervous system. I function dynamically via my brainstem, left hemisphere, and right hemisphere collectively and simultaneously.
SPIRITUAL WELL-BEING	I am a whole spiritual being. I can foster my relational health dynamically via my physical, mental, and emotional experiences collectively and simultaneously.
PERICHORESIS & KENOSIS	I am a dynamic and organic connectome. I continuously integrate and transform my experiences in all areas of my identity, collectively and simultaneously, via self-fulfilling and self-emptying interactions.

DIVINE NATURE	I am Imago Dei regardless of my expression on the identity continuum. I am made in the image of Divinity because of my gender, race, socioeconomic class, ethnicity, age, body type and size, beliefs, degree of faith, intelligence (mental, emotional, physical), ability, and sexual orientation... not in spite of it.
HUMAN/DIVINE EXPRESSIONS	I am a complex expression of gender role(s). I am innately capable of masculine, feminine, and reproductive functions collectively and simultaneously. My identity transcends reductive definitions of gender.
BEHAVIOR	I have a multi-faceted and multi-factorial behavioral network of systems. I am innately capable of thoughts, feelings, and actions collectively and simultaneously.
GENETICS AND EPIGENETICS (NEUROPLASTICITY)	I am a bi-product of my combined nature, nurture, and discipline-based experiences. I am the sum total of both the genetic and epigenetic expressions of every positive and negative experience I have ever had.
SPIRITUAL PRACTICE	I am capable of stillness, solitude, and silence collectively and simultaneously. I have permission and opportunity to pursue self-care via efforts related to internal, local, and global relationships.

EMOTIONAL EXPRESSION	I am a complex emotional being. I develop my own unique emotional landscape via the primitive, complex expressed, and complex control of emotions that I experience collectively and simultaneously.
PROCESSES AND PATHWAYS	I am capable of processing my world via practical, creative, and analytical pathways collectively and simultaneously.
SENSE OF TIME	I experience time in relative context. I am capable of past, present, and future perspectives.
COMMUNICATION STYLE	I am adept in various forms of communication. I am capable of connecting via unintentional and intentional body language as well as verbal communication, collectively and simultaneously.
PERFORMANCE ASSESSMENT STYLE	I am capable of valuing and measuring myself and others by more than the conduct, quality, or quantity of performance(s). I am capable of functioning and assessing my experiences via mechanics, merit, and metrics collectively and simultaneously.

PERSPECTIVE(S)	I am capable of a multitude of viewpoints. I am able to experience, interact with, and observe the world from a nano, micro, and macro perspective collectively and simultaneously.
SELF-AWARENESS	I am capable of various degrees, stages, and states of self-awareness. I experience, interact with, and engage the world second-by-second, moment-by-moment, hour-by-hour, day-by-day, month-by-month, and year-by-year collectively and simultaneously.
SURVIVAL-BASED RESPONSES	I am gifted with and predisposed to a variety of inherent survival-based responses. I have the capacity to produce healthy reactions of: fear/impulsiveness (instinct), attitude/perspective (intuition), and caution/attention (intellect), collectively and simultaneously.
LAW OF THREE	I have the forces of the universe in the fabric of my being. I am capable of demonstrating reconciling, affirming, and restraining forces collectively and simultaneously.

A GLOBAL PERSPECTIVE

When we understand how the brain works, we understand how the Enneagram works. When we understand how the Enneagram works, we understand our identity, and when we understand our identity, we know how to thrive.

This is the essence of the Brain-Based Enneagram™. It is a tool meant for optimal human flourishing. By placing the traditional Enneagram beneath the lens of neuroscience, we are able to engage in personal, relational, and global development and well-being with greater agency, frequency, and awareness. Neuroscience and the Enneagram are two pieces of the same puzzle, and they serve a powerful function when paired together.

Neuroscience tells us that our brains are plastic. They can and do change. Brain anatomy reveals that our operating system is composed of three primary components which mirror the structure of the Enneagram--Brain-stem (instinct triad), Right hemisphere (intuition triad), and Left hemisphere (intellect triad). Functional Neurology shows us how to target areas of the brain in order to physically improve the efficiency of the distinct natures of our identity.

The Enneagram integrates seamlessly. It provides language and definition for the process of development. It opens channels for growth by connecting values and expressions to brain function. It offers a guide for increasing physical, mental, and emotional efficiencies by practically implementing effective methods at effective times in effective ways. The Brain-Based Enneagram™ empowers every human being on the planet to engage with the brain, heal and rebuild after trauma, encourage and strengthen efficiencies, and nourish the relational, integrated nature of our whole identity.

This is true not only on an individual scale, but on a relational and global scale, too. You can apply the same system to your relationships, your business, your governing bodies. The pattern and structure of whole-brain development is reflected in everything you do because the whole-brain is central to everything you do. This is the far-reaching power of the Brain-Based Enneagram™.

CALL FOR CONTINUED RESEARCH AND PROFESSIONAL DIALOGUE

The scope of the content presented in this white paper as well as the magnitude of opportunities that exist for continued refinement and expansion of the Brain-Based Enneagram™ calls for specific scientific research. We understand and expressly state that the methodology and perspectives presented in this text are a dynamic work in progress. The subsequent volumes that will follow this first endeavor will strive to refine, iterate, and expand the content provided thus far. Additionally, our goal is to foster interdisciplinary dialogues within the varied schools of thought within the global Enneagram community and beyond. As such, we welcome any comments, questions, critiques, and professional dialogue that aims to foster the continuing effort of improved health in ourselves, our communities, and the global community at large.

EXTENDED RESOURCES

THRIVE NEURO RESOURCES:

drjerome.com
wholeidentity.com
Thrive NeuroTheology Podcast with Dr. Jerome and Pastor Carl
Thrive NeuroTheology of Self-Care - eCourse
Fear & Safety: The NeuroTheology of Survival

ENNEAGRAM CONTINUING EDUCATION:

enneagraminstitute.com
cynthiabourgeault.org
newyorkenneagram.com
mikemorrell.org
chrisheuertz.com
helenpalmer.com
claudionaranjo.net
enneagramworldwide.com
internationalenneagram.org
enneagramglobalsummit.com
enneagramuserguide.com
drdaviddaniels.com
brenebrown.com/wp-content/uploads/2019/05/List-of-Core-Emotions.pdf

FOR BOOKING INQUIRIES OR ADDITIONAL INFORMATION:

PRIORITIES/MOTIVATIONS

VALUES

⊕ ___ : ________
___ : ________
___ : ________
___ : ________
⊜ ___ : ________
___ : ________
___ : ________
___ : ________
⊖ ___ : ________

TRAVEL ROUTE(S)

WING(S)

⊕ ___ : ________
___ : ________
⊜ ___ : ________
___ : ________
⊖ ___ : ________

IVQ RESULTS

INSTINCTS

___ : ________
___ : ________
___ : ________

RHETI RESULTS

NATURE : SCORES

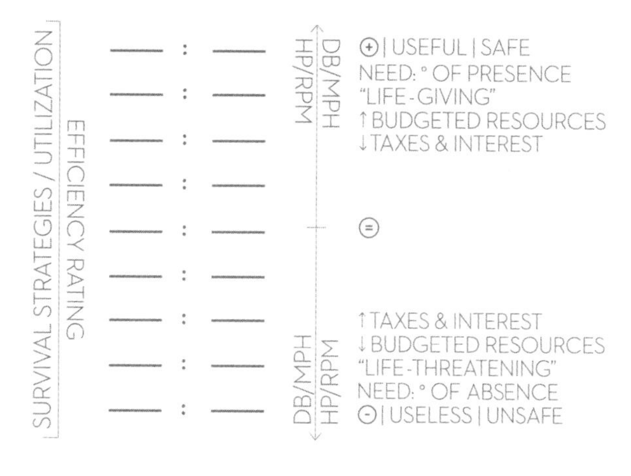

DB: VOLUME, **HP**: STRENGTH,
MPH: SPEED, **RPM**: CAPACITY
⊕ GAS, ⊜ CRUISE, ⊖ BRAKE

POPULATION DENSITY MAP

ALL NINE NUMBERS = GLOBAL
TRIAD = CONTINENT
EACH NUMBER = A COUNTRY
WINGS = FLIGHT PLAN(S)

9 ≻ __W__ : ◯ = %
1 ≻ __W__ : ◯ = %
2 ≻ __W__ : ◯ = %
3 ≻ __W__ : ◯ = %
4 ≻ __W__ : ◯ = %
5 ≻ __W__ : ◯ = %
6 ≻ __W__ : ◯ = %
7 ≻ __W__ : ◯ = %
8 ≻ __W__ : ◯ = %
9

} 100 % YOU

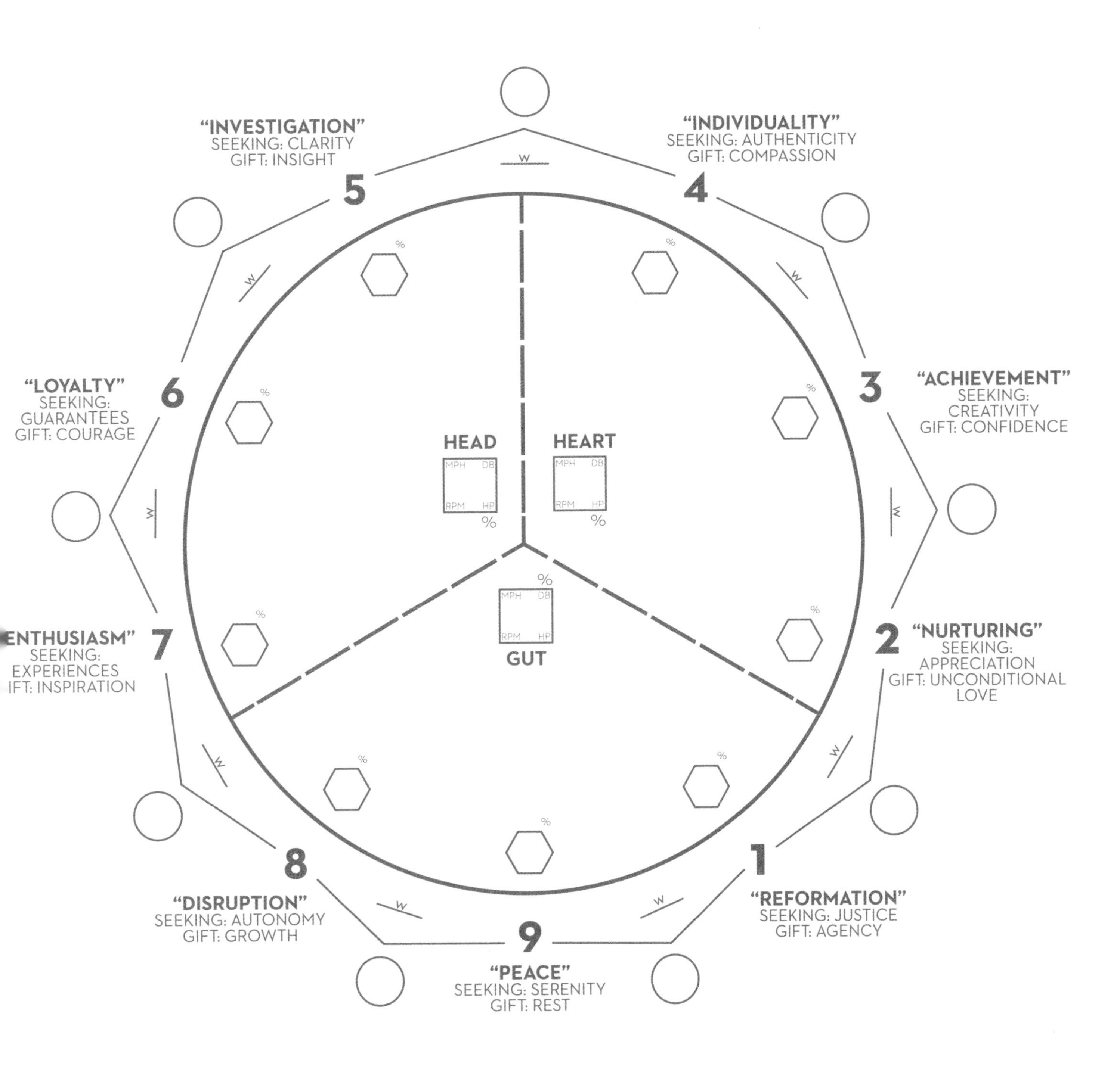
"INVESTIGATION"
SEEKING: CLARITY
GIFT: INSIGHT
5
"INDIVIDUALITY"
SEEKING: AUTHENTICITY
GIFT: COMPASSION
4
"ACHIEVEMENT"
SEEKING:
CREATIVITY
GIFT: CONFIDENCE
3
"LOYALTY"
SEEKING:
GUARANTEES
GIFT: COURAGE
6
HEAD
HEART
MPH
DB
RPM
HP
%
W
ENTHUSIASM"
SEEKING:
EXPERIENCES
IFT: INSPIRATION
7
GUT
"NURTURING"
SEEKING:
APPRECIATION
GIFT: UNCONDITIONAL
LOVE
2
8
"DISRUPTION"
SEEKING: AUTONOMY
GIFT: GROWTH
1
"REFORMATION"
SEEKING: JUSTICE
GIFT: AGENCY
9
"PEACE"
SEEKING: SERENITY
GIFT: REST

5
4
6
3
7
2
8
1
9